The Civil War
from A to Z

Two Points of View

Betty Carlson Kay

authorHOUSE®

AuthorHouse™
1663 Liberty Drive
Bloomington, IN 47403
www.authorhouse.com
Phone: 1-800-839-8640

First published by AuthorHouse 11/30/2010

ISBN: 978-1-4520-9452-6 (e)
ISBN: 978-1-4520-9451-9 (sc)

Library of Congress Control Number: 2010916884

Printed in the United States of America

This book is printed on acid-free paper.

Certain stock imagery © Thinkstock.

Let your "better angels"

always try to see

the other person's

point of view...

With thanks
to Jim Davis, Illinois College professor,
for suggestions and support;
to Laurie and Don Bradley
and Ray Bass
who read this so long ago they probably forgot all about it;
to Sue Ryder Cull
for the diary of her great-great uncles who fought and died
at Gettysburg;
and to David Harmon
of Everhope Plantation.
All photos not otherwise credited are
In the Public Domain
from the Library of Congress.

"In *giving* freedom to the *slave*, we *assure* freedom to the *free*
- honorable alike in what we give and what we preserve. We
shall nobly save, or meanly lose, the last best, hope of earth."

Abraham Lincoln
December 1, 1862
Annual Message to Congress

Introduction

This history of the Civil War encourages young people
to realize that there are two sides to every story.

By presenting each letter of this alphabet of the Civil War
with **two** interpretations,
it is my hope that students will better understand the war
that divided our nation
not so very long ago.

The alphabet may be read in any order one chooses,
although one should probably begin
with Antebellum to set the stage.

At the end, a brief overview
of the years of Reconstruction is added.
President Lincoln's hopes
for a generous peace and reconciliation
unfortunately ended with much controversy.

As this book is read, everyone should realize
the terrible cost of the Civil War
as well as the ideals of the people involved
on both sides of the struggle.

Then, just for fun,
try to imagine
what our country would be like today
if the South had won
the Civil War.

The Civil War from A to Z

A   Antebellum
B   Bull Run
C   Civil War
D   Diaries
E   Election 1860
F   Families
G   Gettysburg
H   Hunley
I   Inauguration
J   John Brown
K   Kansas-Nebraska Act
L   Lee
M   Mercy
N   Nurses
O   Occupation
P   President
Q   Quaker Guns
R   Railroads
S   Secession
T   Tents
U   Uniforms
V   Vicksburg
W   West Point
X   eXchange of Prisoners
Y   Yankees
Z   Zouaves

The Reconstruction Years
Life in Washington City
Chronology of Civil War
Chronology of Abraham Lincoln

Antebellum, North

Antebellum refers to the years before the Civil War in the United States of America. In the North, these were years of growth and change. Farms prospered in many places, yet cities grew with the arrival of immigrants and free blacks from the South. This ready source of workers kept factories humming and laborers bound to work long hours in sometimes poor conditions at the whim of the owner. The economy of the North flourished as the Erie Canal and railroad lines opened doors for selling factory-made products in the western territories, and western farm produce in the East.

Northerners believed in a strong work ethic. Many thought that the free market system could provide wealth to anyone who applied themselves. And though many people did get rich and prospered, the gap between the haves and the have-nots widened as slum living became the norm for the working poor in the Northeast. Child labor laws and the 8-hour workday were far in the future.

The Declaration of Independence declared "...all men are created equal..." and many Northerners believed that this included black men as well as white. Most Northern states were therefore free of slavery by the 1830's. On the other hand, this did not mean that every Northerner wanted black people sitting next to them in church nor working side by side with them. It is important to realize that there were deep prejudices against the black race throughout the free states as well as the slave states making the abolition of slavery a huge challenge. For example, the "free" states of Ohio, Indiana and Illinois did not allow slavery but neither did they welcome free Negroes, going so far as to make black emigration into these states *illegal* (in Illinois until about 1845.)

As children, the Grimke sisters of Charleston, South Carolina, saw slavery first hand on their plantation yet they were surprised as adults to see that "Northern prejudice against color is grinding the colored man to dust in our free states.." Sarah and Angelina Grimke moved to the North and bravely spoke out against slavery in the face of ridicule and violence. The abolition of slavery in the United States was a divisive issue. While the Underground Railroad carried many black passengers to freedom in the North, at the very same time, other Northerners were returning the escapees to their owners in the South according to the Fugitive Slave Laws. And although Northern abolitionists paved the way for black freedom, it was not by any means a universal belief for most of the antebellum years.

"As a nation, we began by declaring that *"all men are created equal"*. We now practically read it, "all men are created equal, *except negroes*." When the Know- Nothings get control, it will read "all men are created equal except negroes and *foreigners and catholics"*. When it comes to this I should prefer emigrating to some country where they make no pretence (sic) of loving liberty- to Russia, for instance, where despotism can be taken pure, without the base alloy of hypocracy. (sic)"
A. Lincoln, Letter to Joshua Speed, August 24, 1855

Antebellum, South

*F*or the lucky few in the Southern states, the Antebellum years meant a wealthy, genteel lifestyle complete with elegant homes and gracious manners. To them the growing country was offering life, liberty and happiness to all, or at least to those that mattered. Cotton was king and wealthy Southerners were like royalty.

But behind this elegance was a not-so-secret secret. The wealth of the few was being made primarily off the labor of the many black slaves who were taken originally from their African homelands and sold as if they weren't really human beings. One out of every three Southerners was a slave by 1860, yet they had no voice in their lives or their futures.

Even though relatively few Southerners actually owned slaves (about 25%), this "peculiar institution" was seen by most as the way to wealth and status and was therefore worthy to be defended. Weren't slaves generously provided with food and clothing from cradle to grave, unlike the Northern poor who were often left homeless and starving in their poverty? Was it not a right of each state to decide if slavery should be allowed? And if some states wanted to allow slavery, shouldn't they be left in peace to do so?

These same arguments over slavery had been causing disagreement among the citizenry since the Revolutionary War. Secession had been threatened more than once in the antebellum years but compromises in 1820 and 1850 had prevented the outbreak of war.

In the South, speech after speech defended a state's right to maintain slavery. In speech after speech in the North, abolitionists interpreted slavery as a sin. This battle of words would not end without a battle of guns. Each side felt it was in the right. Each side was willing to fight for its cause. Each was sure that God was on its side. Determined to teach the other side a lesson, each was willing to sacrifice the lives of thousands of men and women to prove its point.

As the Civil War began, war fever spread on both sides. In her home in Charleston, South Carolina, Mary Chestnut wrote, "The town is crowded with soldiers...they fear the war will be over before they get sight of the fun." Each side was sure that it would be victorious in less than 90 days. How wrong they both were.

Everhope Plantation, Alabama

Everhope Plantation is a classic example of a Greek Revival style plantation house constructed during the antebellum era. Built in 1852 for Captain Nathan Carpenter, a native of North Carolina, the cotton plantation remained in the same family for 122 years. The home is now restored and is listed on the National Register of Historic Places. (Courtesy of David Harmon, Eutaw, Alabama.)

Bull Run, North

$\mathcal{B}$ull Run is the name of a stream near Manassas Junction, Virginia, and the site of the first major battle of the Civil War. Since the Northern Army named its battles after a nearby river or mountain, and the Southern Army named its battles after a nearby city or town, many battles have two names. That is why this battle is called either The Battle of Bull Run or The Battle of First Manassas.

The Armies who met on the battlefield that day had only a few months to prepare for battle. After the firing on Fort Sumter in Charleston Harbor on April 12, 1861, the Yankees and the Rebels had been gathering their forces preparing for a short, easy war. Anticipating that one battle would be all it took to win the war, many Union soldiers signed on for only 90 days. So by July 21, they were ready to head home.

Union leaders warned President Lincoln that they were not yet prepared for a major battle. Lincoln's reply showed his eagerness to act quickly: "You are green, it is true, but they are green also; you are all green alike." So, led by General Irvin McDowell, the Northern Army awoke at 2 a.m. and got a jump on the still sleeping Southerners. With Union victory almost in sight, the tide turned in the afternoon when Union reinforcements were slow to arrive and Southern reinforcements were fast to arrive.

The battleground was only 25 miles from Washington City, close enough for dignitaries and sightseers to travel by carriage to a hill overlooking the battlefield to witness what might just be the only battle of the war. When the disorganized battle became a more disorganized retreat, the roads back to Washington became clogged with fleeing soldiers, tilting wagons and screaming horses jostling with dainty carriages filled with shocked onlookers.

Thus the first major battle of the Civil War was won by the South who, in its own disorganized state, was unable to chase down and defeat the fleeing Union Army. In their retreat, the Northern army realized the difficult task ahead and began to prepare for a long war. Ironically, their humiliation gave them renewed determination to succeed.

Children watching federal soldiers at Bull Run

"Let there be no compromise on the question of *extending* slavery...Have none of it. Stand firm. The tug has to come & better now, than any time hereafter."
A. Lincoln, Letter to Lyman Trumball, December 10, 1860

Bull Run, South

Manassas is the name the South uses for the first major battle of the Civil War. Since a second battle was fought there in 1862, this is correctly called The Battle of First Manassas.

The Southern commander that day in July of 1861 was Pierre G .T. Beauregard, one of their heroes of Fort Sumter. After losing ground in the early morning skirmishes, the outlook was bleak for the Confederate Army. Then, as one weary Confederate general was trying to rally his retreating brigade, reinforcements led by General Thomas J. Jackson arrived to hold the line. The cry went out, "There is Jackson standing like a stone wall! Rally behind the Virginians!" General Jackson received a nickname that day that has stayed with him throughout history: Stonewall Jackson. The Virginian's heroic stand turned the tide and the Southerners fought with renewed vigor.

As the hot midsummer afternoon wore on and the Confederate Army gathered strength, an eerie, piercing scream signaled a surge against the Union line. That Rebel yell so unsettled the Northern troops that they decided they had endured enough for one day. The Great Skedaddle began as the Yankees raced to cross Bull Run, gathering speed as they fled the scene of battle. Jefferson Davis, Confederate President, arrived just in time to witness this victory and urged the rebels to chase the Union Army all the way back to Washington City. However, the Southern disarray in victory was almost as complete as the Union disarray in defeat. Thus, the battle ended there at Manassas, leaving the rebels to gloat, recoup and reorganize.

This first Southern victory filled the Confederacy with confidence which helped to make up for their lack of supplies and manpower. Many battles went their way, especially in the Eastern theater, in the first two years of the "short, easy war" which dragged on and on.

Admiration for General "Stonewall" Jackson spread throughout the South as his reputation grew. The Stonewall Brigade bravely fought in many battles before the general was accidentally shot in the arm by his own men at the Battle of Chancellorsville on May 2, 1863. Fortunately for him, his forces had recently raided Union supply lines and taken a load of medicines including many cases of chloroform to be used as anesthesia during surgeries. As his arm was being amputated with little apparent pain, he said, *"What an infinite blessing.."* was this medicine. After coming out of the anesthesia, he described the experience as …*"the most delightful physical sensation I ever experienced...the most delightful music that ever greeted my ears."* Unfortunately, anesthesia does not prevent complications, and Stonewall Jackson died on May 10, 1863 of pneumonia.

"He has lost his left arm, but I have lost my right."

Robert E. Lee

Civil War, North

Civil War is a war fought between groups of people in the same country. In this case, it was fought between the states in the North and states in the South of the United States of America. When the Southern states said they were seceding from the United States in order to make their own laws and have their own country, President Lincoln insisted that under the United States Constitution there was no provision to leave the Union. To emphasize that point, he rarely referred to "The Confederacy" as a nation because, in his opinion, it did not exist.

The Civil War in the North began as a war to preserve the Union but by 1863 with the Emancipation Proclamation and the acceptance of black troops in the Union army, it became a revolution to overthrow the slavery of the past and to look ahead to what President Lincoln called "a vast future also." He described the Civil War as a struggle to maintain a "government whose leading object is to elevate the condition of men."

But in this terrible struggle, things were quite *un*civilized and the condition of the fighting men was not elevated at all. New technology enabled rifles to shoot straighter, truer and much farther; but the officers still marched their soldiers in formations developed when guns were not as deadly. Thus, brave soldiers found themselves marching straight into a bloodbath as row upon row of soldiers fell in front of entrenched riflemen. New ammunition caused more bodily damage as well. The Civil War became a war of amputations as the only way to save a man's life was to sacrifice a limb.

In this terrible struggle, some battles were fought in mud so deep that the injured had to be propped up against fence posts so they would not drown in the muck. Some battles were fought in a drought so bad that skirmishes were stopped as soldiers fell from thirst and heatstroke. Some battles were fought repeatedly over the same battlefields (especially in Virginia) forcing troops to step over remains of fallen soldiers from previous years. And sometimes, troops fought until both sides were so exhausted that they just stopped fighting and retreated to lick their wounds.

Souvenir cards of the life of a civil war soldier

"Much is being said about peace; and no man desires peace more ardently than I. Still I am yet unprepared to give up the Union for a peace which, so achieved, could not be of much duration."

A. Lincoln, September 12, 1864 Letter to Isaac Schermerhorn

Civil War, South

*I*n the South, the Civil War has several names. Some call it **The War Between the States.** Some call it **The War for Southern Independence.** Some call it **The War of Northern Aggression,** and even **The Recent Unpleasantness.** Whatever it is called, it lasted almost exactly four years and cost the lives of more Americans than all of our other wars combined. Brothers fought against brothers. Whole families joined up, fathers and sons. Some women desperately desired to join the fight, so they dressed as men and successfully hid their femaleness through acts of strength, courage and loose clothing.

It is common to think that all Southerners were for secession and that all Northerners were for reunion. A closer look makes it clear that many people on each side disagreed with their leaders. In the South, there were many Union supporters who remained loyal throughout the war, especially in Appalachia, aiding the Northern troops in any way they could. In the North, so many people wanted the bloodshed to end that they were more than willing to allow the Confederate States to leave the Union. Democrats in the North who wanted an immediate end to the Civil War were nicknamed *Copperheads,* implying that they were like the poisonous snake.

Four years is a long time to remain loyal to a cause during such devastation, death and destruction. It was easy to become disillusioned and many soldiers voted with their feet by simply deserting the battlefields. Desertion reached new highs in 1864. Whole families chose to flee from the raging battlegrounds and instead headed West, opening up a new frontier, new lives and a new era in the history of the United States.

Yet those who remained fiercely loyal to the Southern cause continued to fight to the bitter end. Though shoeless and starving, the piercing Rebel yell could still strike panic in the hearts of the enemy from the North. Proud in defeat as well as in success, the Confederacy wrote an amazing chapter in the history of the United States. It was a defining moment for our country.

Going Into Action

"We are separated because of incompatibility of temper. We are divorced, North from South, because we hate each other so."
Mary Chestnut, Southern diarist

Diaries, North

*D*iaries are personal histories, details of experiences and often the innermost feelings of the writer. During war time people keep diaries not only to record their day-to-day activities, but as a way of dealing with the tragedies unfolding around them.

> *"This is the ninth day of September, 1861. I dedicate this book to my especial use in writing...Though I may be killed, I hope this book may be kept."*

So begins the diary of Alfred Ryder with Company H of the First Michigan Cavalry. By October he was camped near Capitol Hill and wrote home that *"Its (sic) generally healthy but withal there is quite a number sick. Most of the sickness being measles."* In another letter he continues, **"we ... now occupy a position almost in haleing (sic) distance of the Capitals. I can look out now and see its vast unfinished dome over the beautiful grove in front."**

When his brother, John, enlisted, the two brothers wrote home and to each other as they took part in battles from Fredericksburg to Chancellorsville until on June 25, 1863, they met outside the small town of Gettysburg. John's Michigan Iron Brigade and Alfred's First Cavalry camped so near each other that John was able to get a pass to visit Alfred and wrote home on June 28, *"I stayed late at night and had the best visit I ever had in my life talking over old times and what we had passed through in the war. But at last we parted in hopes of meeting again soon."* It was his last letter home. On July 1, John's Iron Brigade met the enemy just outside Gettysburg, and though John and many of the brigade were killed, they are credited with stopping the Confederate advance long enough for the Union Army to gather their forces and prepare to fight another day.

And so it happened that on the fateful day of July 3, Alfred's

Michigan Cavalry thwarted a Confederate rear attack in hand-to-hand combat with sabers. Though the Southern Army was driven back, Alfred was severely wounded and died a week later.

Thus it was with many families. Sons, husbands and fathers fought and died. Families on both sides often lost more than one member. Many, like the Ryder brothers, left a part of themselves in their letters and diaries.

After the exhaustive three day Battle of Gettysburg, the Union army under General Meade failed to chase after the Southern forces, allowing them to cross the Potomac to the safety of Virginia where they would regroup and regain strength. Lincoln, sorely disappointed that the war was not over, penned this letter critical of General George G. Meade, but never sent it:

"Again, my dear general, I do not believe you appreciate the magnitude of the misfortune involved in Lee's escape. He was within your easy grasp, and to have closed upon him would, in connection with our other late successes, have ended the war. As it is, the war will be prolonged indefinitely....Your golden opportunity is gone, and I am distressed immeasureably (sic) because of it."

President Lincoln to Gen George Meade, July 14, 1863

Diaries, South

The Diary of Carrie Berry, a ten-year-old Confederate girl from Atlanta, Georgia, details her life during the famous Burning of Atlanta by Union troops in 1864. By this time, the war was drawing to a close. Vicksburg had fallen. The South had lost at Gettysburg. The Confederates were on their last legs, but still they would not agree to surrender. Union General William T. Sherman decided to convince the South that they should surrender, the sooner the better. He lead his men on a march through the South, destroying buildings, railroads, homes and farms that were in their path. His goal was to end the war once and for all.

Carrie Berry and her family lived in Atlanta. They were staunch Confederates. They wanted the South to win yet they also wanted to live. As the Union army approached Atlanta, Carrie began her diary which is now in the Atlanta History Center. Here are several quotes with Carrie's own spelling and punctuation:

Aug. 3. Wednesday

this is my birthday. I was ten years old, but did not have a cake times were too hard so I celebrated with ironing. I hope by my next birthday we will have peace in our land so that I can have a nice dinner.

Aug 4. Thursday

The shells have ben flying all day and we have stayed in the cellar. Mama put me on (knitting) some stockings this morning and I will try to finish them before school commences.

Aug. 16 Tues.

We had shells all night. There was a large piece came through Mama's room directly after we went to bed and fell on the little bed and I expect if we had been sleeping there some of us would have ben hurt. Cousin Henry and Cousin Eddy came to see us today. They told us that they did not think the Federals would be here much longer to torment us and I hope that it may be so for we are getting very tired of living so.

Sept. 1. Thurs.

...Directly after dinner Cousin Emma came down and told us that Atlanta would be evacuated this evening and we might look for the federals in the morning.

Sept. 3. Sat. 1864

The soldiers have ben coming in all day. ...We have had a rainy day and we all feel gloomy.

Tues. Nov. 15

This has ben a dreadful day. Things have ben burning all around us.

Wed. Dec. 7

I had a little sister this morning at eight o'clock and mama gave her to me (to hold.)

Mon. Jan. 2.

We all started to school this morning to Miss Mattie. Ella, me and Buddie are studying arithmetic, spelling, reading and geography. We are all trying to see which will learn the most.

"So Atlanta is ours, and fairly won."
William Tecumseh Sherman, September 3, 1864

Election 1860, North

Elections for the Presidency of the United States occur every four years but the election of 1860 was perhaps the most crucial ever held. It took place when our country was deeply divided over the issue of state's rights and slavery. Whoever would be elected President would have a great impact on the direction the country would take in the immediate future.

The new Republican Party surprised everyone and nominated Abraham Lincoln, a man who had become known nationally through a series of debates in Illinois with Stephen A. Douglas in 1858. This new political party had strong support in the North as it urged the containment of slavery where it already existed without insisting on complete abolition. The South greatly objected to any restrictions on slavery and promptly labeled the party the Black Republicans. Over and above the slavery issue, Lincoln believed that the most immediate need was in keeping the United States unified as one country. Three other candidates sought the presidency in 1860 as well. Some candidates believed that each state should decide whether to allow slavery or not, potentially spreading slavery into the new territories taking shape out West. Some insisted on strengthening laws allowing slavery to go on forever.

In 1860 it was seen as improper for a candidate to campaign for himself. So friends and supporters did the campaigning for the candidate, relying heavily on newspapers who strongly supported their "favorite son" candidate over the others. Pamphlets were also popular, with a short biography of the candidate and a summary of their platforms. Candidates didn't even attend the convention.

Torchlight parades were perhaps the most impressive form of campaigning in support of Abraham Lincoln. Groups of young men called Wide Awakes marched at night with oil lamps held high. In the darkness, the light from thousands of oil torches along with fireworks overhead made for a very exciting evening. When Lincoln was nominated in August, a daytime parade of floats and an evening parade of Wide Awakes involved 50,000 people in all! It was said to have taken eight hours for the parade to pass the Lincoln home on 8th Street, where the family sat and waved as it went by.

When the election results were in, Lincoln was elected President without carrying a single Southern state, and by receiving less than 40% of the popular vote. The stage was set for the country to decide the issues of union and slavery once and for all.

President Lincoln's First Inaugural - March 4, 1861

"The mystic chords of memory, stretching from every battle-field, and patriot grave, to every living heart and hearthstone, all over this broad land, will yet swell the chorus of the Union, when again touched, as surely they will be, by the better angels of our nature."

A. Lincoln-March 4, 1861 Inaugural Address

Election 1860, South

Electing a President sympathetic to the South was crucial for the politically powerful slave holders in 1860. The widely differing positions of the four candidates were not a surprise to Southerners as they represented the wide range of opinions about slavery in the United States. Some wanted slavery legalized and protected; some wanted it abolished immediately; some wanted it to stay contained and not spread into territories; some wanted to ignore it; but the issue was always slavery.

By this time, eighteen Northern states had made slavery illegal. In countries around the world, from Britain to France to Holland, slavery was already abolished. The South was finding itself isolated within our country and in the world. To keep their "peculiar institution" of slavery alive, they needed to expand into the western territories as well as further south, maybe to Cuba or Mexico or even into Central America! The election of someone unsympathetic to the needs of the South would threaten the whole Southern economy.

Southerners had historically enjoyed national political clout. Their voting block controlled many of the decisions made in the first eighty-five years of our country. They had successfully elected many sympathetic presidents, including James Buchanan, the corrupt, sitting president. Hardly a decision was made in the Congress without the approval of the Southern delegations. But their power was lessening as the country split on the issues surrounding slavery. If the new president would be a Northerner, co-operation in Congress would be impossible, and secession would be the only possible alternative.

Southern Unionists faced a difficult decision. If slave holders insisted on secession, how could they remain loyal to the Union and live in the South? Would they have to fight against their neighbors? In the heat of the moment, it would be dangerous **not** to go along with the strong secessionist movement. The election could bring danger to individuals as well as states.

In the less populated Southern states, with votes split between three candidates (Lincoln was not even on the ballot in most Southern states) the once mighty South could not elect their own choice for President and the election went to the despised Black Republican from the North, Abraham Lincoln. His election left the South with seemingly no choice but to secede to save their beloved way of life.

In this political cartoon, the four candidates for the presidency in 1860 are tearing the country apart. From left to Right, they are: Abraham Lincoln, Stephen A. Douglas, John C. Breckinridge and John Bell.

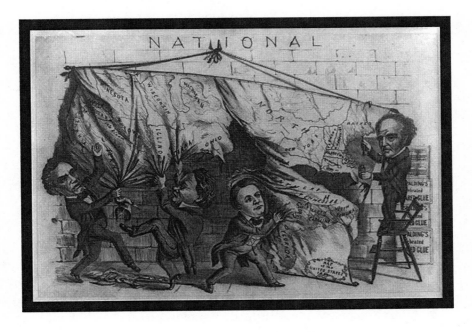

"The election of Mr. Lincoln is undoubtedly the greatest evil that has ever befallen this country. But the mischief is done."
The Richmond Whig, November 6, 1860

Families, North

Families in the North were impacted by the Civil War in several ways depending on their circumstances: whether their family was wealthy or poor, whether they farmed their own land or lived in a teeming city, or whether a family member was in the army. Each of these things made a difference in daily life in the North.

For many, life in the North was unchanged. Wealthy people made fortunes off the war by providing food and provisions to the troops. Primary schools, preparatory schools and colleges were open and many children were able to attend. Fashion conscious New Yorkers shopped at the nation's first department store, A. T. Stewart's, and found five floors of glamour and elegance ... and an elevator!

Yet those who worked in the factories making the goods were usually very poor though working twelve hour days, six days a week. Women increasingly took jobs in the factories as husbands enlisted in the army and were gone for months and years on end. Many children also worked these long hours before child labor laws were enacted. Attending school was not an option for these poor children. Working long hours in cold, dimly lit factories, then returning home to crowded living conditions with no indoor plumbing was not much better than the lives of slaves in the South.

Country families who farmed their own land also worked long days, especially if a father or brothers enlisted in the cause. Then the women and children kept the cows milked, the chickens fed and the crops planted while meeting the challenge of keeping warm in the long winter months. After chores, however, there was a good chance that children continued their schooling. It was expected that children in the North should know how to read and write and schools were open throughout the war. Most children were able to go at least part time, according to the needs of their families.

Surprisingly, some families actually lived in army camps with their fathers! Union officers were allowed to bring their wives to camp and some also brought their children. This photograph of a Pennsylvania family shows how they lived in camp when their father was not in battle. Mother did the cooking and the laundry, took care of the baby and nursed any wounds. Look closely- they even brought their dog!

Some families joined the war effort by living in camp with their officer father. Here the 31st Pennsylvanians are joined by a family, complete with baby and even a dog!

Families, South

Families in the South had quite a different experience. Since the families lived on the land where most of the battles were fought for four years, young children witnessed the war first hand and experienced the terror of violence close to home.

Wealthy Southern families tried to keep a semblance of order in their daily lives. Often, the plantation owner did not join the army, opting to stay at home to keep an eye on the slaves working the fields. The food they produced was greatly needed by soldiers and civilians alike. Their privileged children would have kept up with tutors at home for at least part of the war. By the end of the conflict, however, with no slaves to work the land, everyone did what he or she had to do to stay alive including helping in the fields and cooking.

Poorer Southern families faced a terrible four years on their little plots of land. Just feeding their families became the focus of all their efforts. Elementary education had not been universally offered to poor white children in the South and school became out of the question as everyone was needed to help families survive. With almost all the men and boys enlisted, women and children were left on their own with little resources. As starvation spread throughout the South, letters were filled with pleas to husbands to leave the army and come home to help their families. Torn between loyalty to the Southern cause and loyalty to their families, many fathers chose their families. Some families then left the South altogether and joined the great westward migration where there was still hope for the future.

After the War, when the Freedman's Bureau established schools in the South for freed slave children, it also included poor white children who had been left uneducated all too often before and during the war.

Wartime Moves

Families moved from place to place during the war. Some moved from North to South and some moved from South to North, depending on their loyalties. Some were disillusioned by the fighting and moved out west to start a new life without the threat of war.

(Note woman smoking corncob pipe.)

Gettysburg, North

Gettysburg was a prosperous little town near the Pennsylvania / Maryland border. It was the hub of several crossroads and unexpectedly became a crossroad of the Civil War. For during the first week of July in 1863, its peace was shattered by a huge three-day battle which forever linked its name to the triumph and horror of war.

At the end of June,1863, Union scouts were watching as scattered units of Rebel soldiers headed North into Pennsylvania. Alert Northern troops excitedly marched double time to cut them off and protect Federal soil. On June 30, groups of Yanks and Rebs literally bumped into each other outside of Gettysburg. Both sides were exhausted from miles of marching in the hot summer sun; their commanding officers where not yet present; and they had no orders to fight there. Yet, this first, small skirmish grew as fellow soldiers on each side joined in the battle.

The leader of the Army of the Potomac, General George Meade, had been in charge only a few days when major fighting broke out on the morning of July 1. But for the tenacious stand of troops like the Iron Brigade, the South might have won a big psychological victory that day. As it was, General Lee waited for **his** reinforcements, giving the North time to gather **their** reinforcements, which saved the biggest, bloodiest battles for the following days.

And so it was that for three days battles raged in the Peach Orchard, Seminary Ridge, Little Round Top and Cemetery Ridge. Good decisions and bad decisions were made by excited officers. Each side had moments of attacking too early or attacking too late. The battles ebbed and flowed. Heroism and cowardice, injury and death played their parts on those long, hot days.

When it was all over on the Fourth of July, the Union celebrated a grand victory. The defeated but not beaten Army of Northern Virginia retreated across the Potomac in pouring rain. The little town of Gettysburg was left to finish burying the dead and nurse the dying, even as an eerie peace settled over the misty Pennsylvania countryside. Those who lived there knew that life in Gettysburg had been forever changed.

Cemetery Gatehouse, July 1863

During the battle of Gettysburg, several soldiers noticed a sign posted in Evergreen Cemetery on Cemetery Hill south of town. It read:

**All persons found using firearms in these grounds will
be persecuted with the utmost rigor of the law.**

The soldiers found this humorous since the cemetery grounds were obviously filled with a wide variety of firearms!

THE GETTYSBURG ADDRESS

DELIVERED
BY
ABRAHAM
LINCOLN
NOV. 19 1863

AT THE
DEDICATION
SERVICES
ON THE
BATTLE FIELD

Fourscore and seven years ago our fathers brought forth on this continent a new nation, conceived in liberty, and dedicated to the proposition that all men are created equal. * * * Now we are engaged in a great civil war, testing whether that nation, or any nation so conceived and so dedicated, can long endure. * * We are met on a great battle-field of that war. * We have come to dedicate a portion of that field as a final resting place for those who here gave their lives that that nation might live. * * It is altogether fitting and proper that we should do this. * * But in a larger sense we cannot dedicate, we cannot consecrate, we cannot hallow this ground. * The brave men, living and dead, who struggled here, have consecrated it far above our poor power to add or detract. The world will little note, nor long remember, what we say here, but it can never forget what they did here. * * It is for us, the living, rather to be dedicated here to the unfinished work which they who fought here have thus far so nobly advanced It is rather for us to be here dedicated to the great task remaining before us, that from these honored dead we take increased devotion to that cause for which they gave the last full measure of devotion; * that we here highly resolve that these dead shall not have died in vain; that this nation, under God, shall have a new birth of freedom, and that the government of the people, by the people, and for the people, shall not perish from the earth

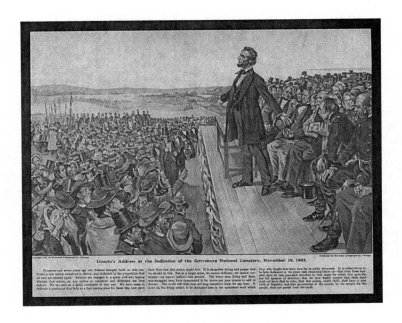

President Abraham Lincoln was asked to say a few words at the dedication of the cemetery at the Gettysburg battlefield on November 19, 1863, after the main speaker, Edward Everett had spoken. "It is the desire that, after the Oration, you, as Chief Executive of the nation, formally set apart these grounds to their sacred use by a few appropriate remarks," wrote David Wills of the cemetery committee.

Lincoln's well-thought-out words were delivered in his famous high pitched voice in under three minutes after Everett had spoken for two hours. Lincoln was finished before most people had begun to pay attention, and before the photographers had completed their set up. Afterwards, Everett complimented the President on his speech and Lincoln replied that he was pleased that it was not a total failure. His disappointment probably had to do with the fact that he was not feeling well.

Actually, he was coming down with a variety of smallpox and spent the next three weeks under quarantine in the White House. Joking about his contagious illness and his inability to meet the constant demands of office-seekers, Lincoln is remembered as saying, " Now I have something I can give everybody."

Gettysburg, South

Gettysburg was the South's best chance for a big victory on Northern soil. Another Confederate victory after their recent win at Chancellorsville could mean the end of this War of Northern Aggression. Success in Pennsylvania could mean increased respect for the Southern cause in England and France. Those countries might then recognize the Confederacy as a nation and send aid.

In June of 1863, Robert E. Lee's Army of Northern Virginia was on a roll even as they were running low on food, supplies and guns. It was now or never for this increasingly desperate army. Energized rebel troops were eager to follow Lee onto Northern soil where lush farmlands were still yielding food just right for the taking. Besides, Gettysburg was said to have a supply of shoes which the Southerners desperately needed. Too many rebels were marching barefooted.

Communicating with thousands of Confederates as they made their way North was challenging. Scouts and couriers did their best to co-ordinate plans, but as it happened, the battle began before everyone was in place and ready. Not even Robert E. Lee was present when the fighting began!

As two hot July days went by, the battles continued to go first one way and then the other. Lee became more and more eager to make a bold attack and settle this once and for all. To the dismay of some of his Generals, including James Longstreet, Lee ordered an attack on July 3 which would be the grand and glorious end of the Union army. This mile-wide band of thousands of proud Southerners marching across the field straight into the guns of the ready-and-waiting Northern soldiers became known as Pickett's Charge. It was breath taking to see 14,000 flag waving, courageous rebels marching in formation and it was shocking to realize that in only thirty minutes, less than half returned to the Southern lines. The Southern army retreated across the Potomac River in pouring rain fully expecting Northern soldiers to follow them and destroy the remaining army. But the Union army was badly damaged as well. Yes, the North had won a magnificent victory but they were too exhausted to chase the enemy down to their final defeat. Not

Longstreet at Gettysburg, July 2, 1863.

knowing that on the same July 4, 1863 Vicksburg had also fallen into Northern hands, Lee led his exhausted army safely home to Virginia where they spent time recovering from their near disaster in the North. Lee took full responsibility for the loss at Gettysburg and offered his resignation with these words:

"Dear President Davis,
I cannot even accomplish what I myself desire. How can I fill the expectations of others? I generally feel a begrowing failure of my bodily strength. I anxiously urge the matter upon your excellency for my belief that a younger and abler man than myself can be readily obtained."
His request was denied.

Hunley, North

The $\mathcal{H}$unley was only a small blip in the big picture of the naval superiority of the North which was obvious from the very beginning of the Civil War. With many more ships and sailors, the Union Navy was able to advance on two fronts at the same time: the long ocean coastline from Virginia to New Orleans <u>and</u> the Mississippi River system, control of which would split the Confederacy in two.

Since the South, lacking a large navy, fought from land not sea, the coastline fighting along the Atlantic seaboard and the Gulf of Mexico had mostly to do with controlling ports and blockading Southern ships trying to sneak through the Federal lines to buy and sell goods. As the superior Federal Navy tightened the noose around the Southern ports, the besieged Confederates found themselves desperate for supplies of ammunition, food, clothing and shoes. In the dead of night, private blockade runners made daring runs through the patrols to bring aid to the south and riches to their own pockets. Over 1500 blockade runners were captured in the course of the war by Northern ships who then got to divvy up a large portion of the captured supplies.

Equally important was the war being waged on the Mississippi River system in the heart of the country. Working together, the Union Army and Navy forces used heavily armored river boats, a few with turning turrets, who could attack from the river while the foot soldiers attacked from land. Leading the Union army as the Federals pushed south was a little known Brigadier-General named Ulysses S. Grant. His Union forces heading South and the Union forces heading North under the command of Flag Officer David Farragut, believed that between the two of them, they would control the river, splitting the Confederacy in two and speeding the end of the war.

Yet all the mighty power of the Union Army and Navy had a

monumental struggle to conquer the Confederates who were making a desperate last stand high on the bluffs above Vicksburg, Mississippi. Their hillside advantage point allowed them to repel Federal attacks repeatedly. The South's stubborn determination lead to a siege which caused much hardship and took many lives. When Vicksburg surrendered on the Fourth of July in 1863, Union forces soon regained control of the Mississippi River, severely limiting the strength of the Confederacy.

Deck and turret of U.S.S. Monitor seen from the bow
James River, Virginia

"Let us have faith that right makes might, and in that faith, let us, to the end, dare to do our duty as we understand it."
A. Lincoln February 27, 1860 Cooper Institute Address

Hunley, South

Horace Hunley helped develop a submarine designed to sink Union ships blockading Charleston Harbor. A loyal Confederate to the core, Hunley was a Louisiana lawyer with money to invest in a scheme which would terrorize the Union vessels which were preventing food, clothing and ammunition from reaching the increasingly desperate people of Charleston, South Carolina.

From the beginning the tiny sub seemed plagued with bad luck. It was powered by human rowers who sat hunched over, cranking a heavy shaft for hours on end, only to return exhausted and without having encountered a wooden vessel within firing range. Two seven-man crews (including Hunley himself) had already drowned in the submarine before the night of February 17, 1864, when it made its first and only successful run.

On that night the USS *Housatonic* was anchored outside the Charleston Harbor, a distance of about 4 miles for the rowers. Though the ship's watch saw something surface a few yards away and sounded the alarm, the sub was already close enough to ram a spar into her wooden side. The rowers immediately reversed their cranking, pulling on the spar which detonated with enough force to blow a large hole into the doomed ship.

After the explosion, all the *Hunley* crew had to do was row back to safety, but they never made it. For years there was speculation about their last hours, until finally in 1995, the sub was discovered under three feet of silt near the spot where she sank the *Housatonic*. Raising her took teamwork and great skill. Opening the submarine found the sailors still positioned at their posts. Today, restoration work continues on the world's first successful submarine, which will be housed in a museum for all to see.

There were different opinions of this new stealth weapon, depending on whose side one was on. The Confederates saw it as a clever and timely weapon. However, Union Admiral John Dahlgren declared that captured submariners should be hanged "for using an engine of war not recognized by civilized nations."

The Hunley, in sketch and in diagrams.
(Courtesy of Naval History and Heritage Command)

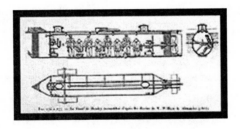

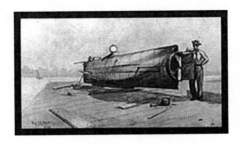

Inauguration, North

*I*nauguration is the formal start of something new. Every four years after a president is elected, he gives an Inaugural Address at his Inauguration. In 1860, when Abraham Lincoln was elected President of the United States, he knew his Inaugural Address would be his most important speech to date. He had won the presidential election without carrying *one single* state in the South. Even before his Inauguration on March 4,1861, seven states had seceded from the Union, and more were threatening to join them. Lincoln knew his Inaugural Address was one last chance to convince secessionists that there was still time to settle their grievances without war. This speech could make a difference in the future of the United States of America. He prepared it, practiced it and polished it.

Lincoln knew the power of words and the joy of writing convincingly. Here he used both reason and emotion to plead his case for taking adequate time to consider the consequences of hasty actions. He told the disgruntled Southerners " In your hands,...and not in mine, is the momentous issue of civil war." But already actions were set into motion, and what he called "the better angels of our nature" didn't stand a chance.

And so the war came.

Four years later, in a much shorter but eloquent Second Inaugural Address on another March 4th, there was no lengthy plea for union. Four long, heartbreaking years of war had taken their toll. The end was finally in sight. Physically worn down, Lincoln rose up... up above feelings of hatred and bitterness to compassion and healing. He thought of the widows and fatherless children, both in the North and in the South. He thought of the soldiers who now were missing an arm or a leg. He thought of those who had lost a beloved son, even as the Lincoln family had lost their son Willie. He had presided over four long years of war. Now the President looked forward to presiding over four years of peace. Little could he know.

"With malice toward none; with charity for all; with firmness in the right, as God gives us to see the right, let us strive on to finish the work we are in; to bind up the nation's wounds; to care for him who shall have borne the battle, and for his widow, and his orphan........."
A. Lincoln, March 4, 1865 Second Inaugural Address

The Second Inaugural

Lincoln/Johnson campaign medals of 1864

Inauguration, South

Jefferson Davis actually had two inaugurations to be the President of the Confederacy. On February 18, 1861, Davis was sworn in as the President of the *provisional* Confederate government which was just beginning to take shape. The ceremony took place on the portico of the state house in Montgomery, Alabama. With dignified bearing and a far-reaching voice, Davis reminded the crowd that nothing less than the Declaration of Independence proclaimed that government rested on the consent of the governed as well as their right to revolution. In 1776 Americans had believed in this right of revolution and fought a war against England to achieve their freedom. Now the South was doing the same thing.

As the band played a new song called "Dixie", a proud Southerner named William Yancey foresaw destiny and declared, "The man and the hour have met." To be honest, however, Jefferson Davis would have preferred a military position.

The second inaugural of Jefferson Davis took place in February 1862 in front of the statue of George Washington in the new Confederate capital of Richmond, Virginia. Now Jefferson Davis was being sworn in as the President of the *permanent* Confederate government. Again, Davis likened the Southern struggle for self-government to the Revolutionary War. This inaugural took place on the heels of several devastating Southern losses including the one at Fort Donelson, Tennessee, where 13,000 Southern troops surrendered to a little known Northern officer named Ulysses S. Grant.

Being deeply religious, Davis believed in the Providence of God, who favors a cause that is just. Thus, Jefferson Davis, President of the Confederate States of America, never doubted that God was on the side of the South.

THE STARTING POINT OF THE GREAT WAR BETWEEN THE STATES.
INAUGURATION OF JEFFERSON DAVIS

Inauguration of Jefferson Davis
Montgomery, Alabama
February 18, 1861

John Brown, North

John Brown took center stage in the American experience at the arsenal in Harper's Ferry, Virginia, in 1859 as the country was ready to erupt in violence. Imagine the United States as a volcano, boiling with controversy. The lava had been churning since before the Revolution of 1776 with the unresolved issue of slavery. Insistent slave owners, zealous abolitionists, unsatisfactory compromises, and the Fugitive Slave Law kept the lava simmering just below the boiling point. It wouldn't take much for it to overflow.

Enter the Northerner John Brown, an anti-slavery fanatic and a dreamer. His violent side had already shown itself in skirmishes in Kansas Territory. He fed his abolitionist fury on stories of guerrilla warfare and envisioned himself arming a righteous slave rebellion. He believed that slaves would throng to him in a huge uprising, a glorious moment that never materialized. Instead, after easily overtaking the arsenal in Harper's Ferry, Brown and his few men found themselves surrounded by townspeople and militia. By evening the U.S. Marines had arrived. They were led that day by Colonel Robert E. Lee who brought the scene under control in a few moments. Brown was captured and ordered to stand trial in Virginia.

The trial which followed was that of a frail, ailing old man who defiantly insisted he was acting out of a higher calling by attempting to free the slaves. His eloquence inspired some Northerners to believe him a martyr to the abolition cause, justifying his lawlessness. When he was hanged on December 2, 1859, many Northern church bells tolled, salutes were fired, and people bowed in a moment of silence, while at the same time some called the attempt the work of a madman.

Brown's raid was even put to an old tune, and when Northern soldiers marched off to battle in 1861, they tramped along singing,

"John Brown's body lies a mould'ring in the ground".
John Brown's body lies a mould'ring in the ground,
John Brown's body lies a mould'ring in the ground,
But his soul goes marching on."

Julia Ward Howe was visiting army camps when she heard the men singing this mournful tune, and she was inspired to write her own more uplifting words for it. Thus, her "The Battle Hymn of the Republic" became one of the finest marching songs of all time.

John Brown's Insurrection

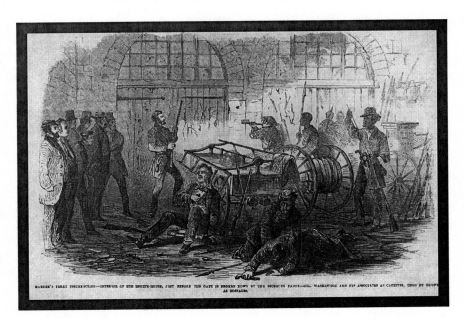

"John Brown's effort was peculiar. It was not a slave insurrection.
It was an attempt by white men to get up a revolt among
slaves, in which the slaves refused to participate."
A. Lincoln, at Cooper Institute, February 27, 1860

John Brown, South

John Brown encouraged a slave uprising, knowing full well that Southerners lived in terror of such a rebellion. On plantations far and wide black slaves outnumbered their white masters. Recognizing these odds, slave owners liked to believe that their own slaves were so content and so well treated that they would never rebel. Yet over the years there had been a few uprisings and a disturbing number of runaway slaves; so the fear of violence could easily strike panic into the hearts of even the most well armed masters.

Southerners would never forget the Nat Turner Rebellion of 1831. Nat was an intelligent slave who was also prone to having visions and seeing signs from God. These visions told him to rise up and throw off his masters. With a small group of trusted friends, Nat led an attack that eventually killed at least 55 white people in Virginia. Nat was caught and hanged with some other conspirators. In the hysteria that followed, at least 200 black slaves were killed by white mobs throughout the South.

With this threat ever present, Southerners panicked when John Brown attempted to stir up a great slave rebellion on October 16, 1859, at Harper's Ferry, Virginia. Never mind that it failed miserably and that it never attracted any slaves into rebellion. Even though Brown was immediately caught and sentenced to death, Southerners grew more hostile toward all Yankees. Some Northerners living in the South were coated with tar and feathers and several were lynched. Others feared for their lives and fled the South. Northerners who disagreed with Brown far outnumbered those who supported his violent attempt at a slave rebellion. While Abraham Lincoln agreed with Brown that slavery was wrong, he insisted "that cannot excuse violence, bloodshed and treason."

After he was hanged on December 2, 1859, the ghost of John Brown seemed to walk the land. Southerners joined military companies and prepared to defend their hearth and home. As tensions rose, the country also prepared for the presidential election of 1860.

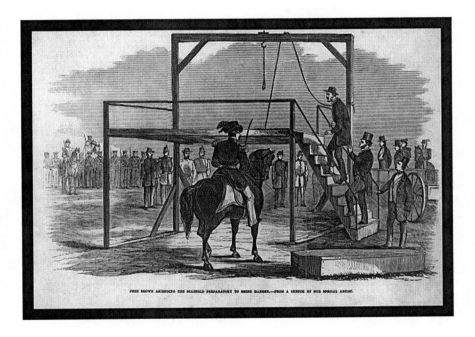

JOHN BROWN ASCENDING THE SCAFFOLD PREPARATORY TO BEING HANGED.—FROM A SKETCH BY OUR SPECIAL AGENT.

Though he said nothing from the gallows, John Brown
handed a note to the executioners which said,

"I, John Brown, am now quite certain that the crimes of this
guilty land will never be purged away but with blood."

Kansas-Nebraska Act, North

Kansas Territory in the 1850's was the focus of the struggle between the pro-slavery forces and abolitionists. The Missouri Compromise of 1820 had seemingly decided the slavery issue long ago...slavery would NOT be allowed to spread into the territories above the 36° 30' latitude. Northerners were pleased that slavery would be restricted. Then, in 1854, the Kansas-Nebraska Act was passed which allowed the territories *themselves* to decide if they would be slave or free. Thus, Kansas Territory was set up for bloody conflict as each side tried to win the most votes. Proslavery men crossed from Missouri into Kansas by the thousands to vote to allow slavery, while Northern abolitionists moved into "KT" to claim it as free soil. Obviously, fraudulent voting was going on, leading to violence.

In Illinois the Kansas-Nebraska Act and the violent reactions to it stirred the heart and mind of an eloquent prairie lawyer who put pen to paper and spoke his mind. Abraham Lincoln knew that the current Senator from Illinois, Stephen A. Douglas, had been instrumental in getting the Kansas-Nebraska Act passed. Lincoln decided that he would run for the Senate against Douglas on the grounds that there was a basic law of decency that overrode the right of an individual territory to decide an issue such as slavery. This law was the "inalienable right to life, liberty and the pursuit of happiness," as guaranteed in the Constitution to all citizens.

In his now famous speech on June 16, 1858 accepting the nomination to be the Republican candidate for the senate seat, Lincoln predicted a great crisis was looming ahead for the nation:

"In *my* opinion, it *will* not cease, until a *crisis* shall have been reached, and passed. "A house divided against itself cannot stand."

I believe this government cannot endure, permanently half *slave* and half *free*. I do not expect the Union to be *dissolved* - I do not expect the house to *fall* - but I *do* expect it will cease to be divided. It will become all one thing or the other."

Lincoln won the popular vote, but lost the election which was decided in the state legislature. Yet his words resonated with his fellow citizens in the North and set his life on a new path for the future. In the 1860 presidential election, the contest over territories was a defining issue.

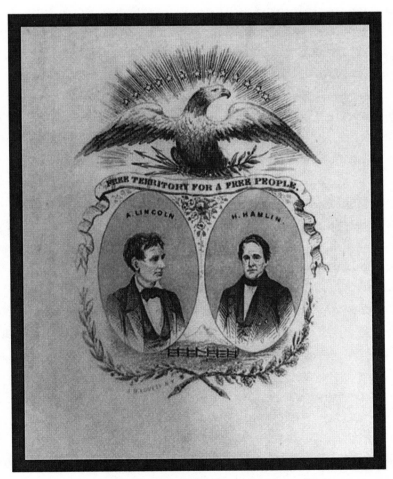

Free territories out west became the rallying cry of the Republican Party in 1860.

Kansas-Nebraska Act, South

Southerners were enthusiastic to gain power in the U.S. Senate by increasing the number of slave states. The addition of Florida and Texas gave them the upper hand in 1845, but why stop there? They had their eyes on Mexico and even Cuba and far-away Nicaragua! Additional slave states would increase Southern political strength against the North which was growing in population and technology.

At the same time, the vast Kansas-Nebraska Territory was luring settlers ever west. Southerners insisted that it be open to slaveholder and non-slaveholder alike. Dividing the territory in two looked like a way to keep the delicate balance; Kansas could be a slave territory and Nebraska, a free territory. However, this went against the Compromise of 1820 which had stood for many years. Though Southerners were pleased when the Kansas-Nebraska Bill passed, they knew that enforcing it would not be easy.

The Southern path to success involved outnumbering the antislavery people in Kansas. Since Missouri was close by, it was easy to gather a group of men who would ride over the border and vote for the proslavery candidates and a proslavery constitution. "Missourians have nobly defended our rights," said an Alabama newspaper of this illegal activity. It was then just an easy step for these "Border Ruffians" to turn violent against the abolitionists who lived in the Kansas town of Lawrence, killing several men.

"The admission of Kansas into the Union as a slave state is now a point of honor" wrote South Carolina Congressman Preston Brooks, who later beat Massachusetts Senator Charles Sumner with a cane until the antislavery speaker collapsed in his Senate desk. Southern newspapers praised this attack in defense of Southern honor and many sent Brooks gifts of more canes.

The attack on Charles Sumner as well as the attack on Lawrence, Kansas ignited a terrible rage in an abolitionist zealot named John Brown who had moved to Kansas to defend it from proslavery forces. "We must fight fire with fire" and "strike terror into the hearts of the proslavery people" he told his men. To even the score, he figured they needed to slay five proslavery men- which they did on the night of May 24, 1856. The five men killed on Pottawatomie Creek that night had nothing to do with the Lawrence murders. Yet Brown declared it, "An eye for an eye".

Kansas Territory was basically lawless. The US Army had too few troops to stop such bush-whacking, and though Brown went unpunished, these deaths in Bloody Kansas directly influenced the start of the Civil War.

Political Cartoon

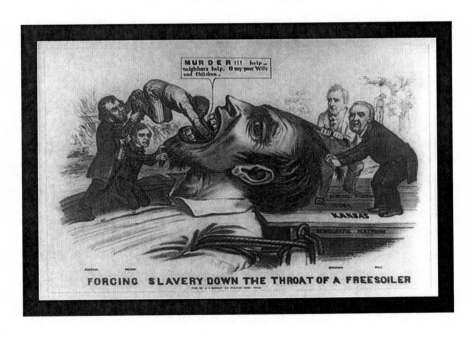

Lee, Robert Edward, North

*L*ee was a traitor in the eyes of Northerners, simple as that. He had served the United States Army for 32 years as an engineer, as a soldier in the Mexican War, and as Superintendent of West Point. His decision to decline the offer of leadership of the Union Army in the Civil War meant that he would fight against his country in defense of his state of Virginia even though he wrote:"...I do not believe in secession as a constitutional right, nor that there is sufficient cause for revolution." Siding with the South made him a traitor to the United States.

As soon as the war began, Robert E. Lee was asked to lead the Federal army. He was 54 years old, in apparent good health, well liked and respected. He had demonstrated excellent leadership skills as well. But when Virginia seceded, he felt he could not take up arms against his state and decided instead to accept a position in the Confederate forces. Although he had studied warfare as a student at West Point and understood war tactics, he had never lead troops into battle and he faced a steep learning curve. As the war went on, he learned from his mistakes and by the spring of 1862, he took the reins of leadership for the Army of Northern Virginia. Lee's name became legendary. It could strike fear in the hearts of Union troops as, outnumbered and outgunned, he could still pull off a victory or a hasty retreat, prolonging the war.

Robert E. Lee never owned a home but his wife, Mary Custis Lee, owned an estate in Arlington, Virginia, just across the Potomac River from Washington City. Mary Custis Lee was the great-granddaughter of Martha Custis Washington, wife of President George Washington. The estate had a grand view of the capitol and the Washington Monument which was slowly rising from the ground. Yet Northerners felt entitled to this property which was filled with mementoes of the first President of the United States. Hard feelings toward the Confederate Lees showed when Northern troops took over the Arlington estate soon after Mary and her family left for the relative safety of Richmond. It was not long before the property became a hallowed Union cemetery, much to the frustration of Mrs. Lee who always saw it as HER home which she never stopped trying to reclaim.

Today the Custis-Lee Mansion and the surrounding cemetery are important reminders of our country's history. Visiting it teaches citizens about the complex history of both the Revolutionary War and the Civil War.

Arlington House, 1864

"It is well that war is so terrible lest we grow too fond of it."
R.E. Lee, December 13, 1862, Battle of Fredericksburg

Lee, Robert Edward, South

*L*ee was a beloved hero, just about achieving sainthood in the eyes of the people of the Confederacy. But Robert E. Lee did not see himself as a hero at all. And he certainly didn't see himself as the traitor portrayed in the North! Rather, he saw himself as leading a Second Revolutionary War. His father, Lighthorse Harry Lee had fought to free the young United States from the oppression of England back in 1776. In 1861, Lee believed he was defending the South from similar oppression from the North.

But long before he was praised, Lee was ridiculed by his own troops. When Lee alone predicted a long drawn out war, he disappointed Southerners who thought they would lick the Yankees in ninety days flat. When he did not take the offensive as soon as some wanted, he was nicknamed "Granny Lee." When he ordered the men to dig trenches to protect Richmond, he was taunted by the nickname "King of Spades".

So it was that admiration and trust in Lee grew slowly but surely. As he became more daring, even attacking the North at Gettysburg, soldiers and civilians alike stood by him in victory and defeat. The tears of his fellow Confederates at the surrender at Appomattox were for the defeat of their hero as well as the defeat of the southern way of life.

In the years after the war, people flocked to be in his presence. He could not take a walk without some well-wisher joining him. Always a very shy man, he was at a loss as to what to say to these fans. Asked to be the president of Washington College in Lexington, Virginia, he accepted the position and his fame boosted the enrollment and donations at the school.

Robert E. Lee, the peacemaker, encouraged cooperation with the victorious Union army. He discouraged violence that erupted during the Reconstruction years. He believed that the South could and should return to the status quo of the antebellum years, which for him included white superiority in politics, government and economics. It disappointed him that the country had changed so much from the life he had loved. It saddened him that his wife, Mary, never regained her treasured Arlington estate.

Robert and Mary are buried at his beloved college which is now renamed Washington and Lee University in his honor.

"I can anticipate no greater calamity for the country than the dissolution of the Union. It would be an accumulation of all the evils we complain of and I am willing to sacrifice everything but honor for its preservation."
Robert E. Lee

Mercy, North

Mercy was perhaps shown most consistently in the Civil War by Abraham Lincoln himself. Always a kind man, Lincoln had the ability to see the world through another person's eyes and feel their pain.

During the long, four year war, there were many times when Lincoln showed mercy to soldiers. In fact, he so often showed mercy that some Generals thought he was undermining their discipline. For example, Lincoln pardoned a young blue coat who fell asleep on guard duty and was sentenced to death by firing squad. Lincoln told a friend, "I could not think of going into eternity with the blood of this poor young man on my skirts."

Another time, two dozen soldiers had been sentenced to death for desertion. Lincoln refused to sign the orders saying, "There are already too many weeping widows in the United States. For God's sake don't ask me to add to the numbers, for I won't do it."

In 1862, Lincoln also showed mercy to Native Americans during the Sioux uprising in Minnesota. Treaties with the Indians had worked to the advantage of the white population and the Indian agents more than the Indian population, leaving the Sioux unable to feed themselves. A group of young warriors raided a farm to get food for their starving tribe and in the skirmishes that followed, several hundred settlers were killed. After the uprising, over 300 Indians were to be hanged from the largest gallows ever built in Mankato, Minnesota.

Lincoln could not believe that so many were guilty of horrendous crimes. He carefully studied the list of Indian names and their offenses and reduced the number to be hanged. On December 26, 1862, 38 Sioux Indians were hanged in the largest one day execution in American history. However, showing mercy to Indians was not a popular idea and the governor of the state of Minnesota actually told President

Lincoln that if he would hang more Indians he'd get more votes in the next election.

Although such decisions were often difficult
and unpopular, Lincoln said,
"I have always found that mercy bears richer fruits than strict justice."
Attributed to A. Lincoln in *Lincoln Memorial, 1882, Osborn Oldroyd, (ed.)*

Mercy, South

Mercy often goes unseen. Small acts of compassion take place daily without calling attention to themselves. Yet even in times of war, impressive acts of mercy stand out amid the brutality.

Take, for example, Richard Kirkland at the Battle of Fredericksburg, Virginia, on December 13, 1862. His unit from South Carolina was hunkered down behind a stone wall at the base of Marye's Heights. They had a safe, protected view of thousands of Union soldiers charging towards them across "No Man's Land" in long, unprotected rows. In a very short time, eight thousand Union soldiers were mowed down and then left all night on the field right where they had fallen.

It was pure torture for Richard to listen to their cries for help during that endless night. In the morning light the scene of the disabled and dying bodies writhing right before his very eyes was too much for him to bear. Yesterday, they were enemies. Today, they were wounded, suffering men. His code of honor required action.

So Sgt. Kirkland borrowed canteens, filled them with fresh water and slowly crawled over the protective stone wall. As he began offering drinks of water to the thirsty, miserable soldiers, his rebel friends held their breath, sure that he would be shot by the Federal sharpshooters who were carefully watching from not so very far away. Instead, Richard heard cheers as soldiers on both sides appreciated his bravery and compassion and held their fire. He made several safe trips with refilled canteens before the battle resumed.

For this act of mercy Kirkland was immortalized on this handsome memorial as The Angel of Marye's Heights. He died later at the battle of Chickamauga, September 20, 1863.

**The Monument to Sergeant Richard Kirkland,
The Angel of Marye's Heights.**

(Photo in author's collection)

Nurses, North

*N*urses played an important role in the health care system in the Civil War. At the beginning of the war hospitals were simply field tents, nearby churches or large homes. There was no system for caring for soldiers where they fell nor was there a system for getting the injured off the battlefields, except for the good intentions of fellow comrades. As injuries mounted, the first ambulance corps was put into place to provide for evacuation and care before the soldiers were carried to hospitals. The US Sanitary Commission formed and gave all the paid positions to men. Soon tens of thousands of women volunteers joined the organization in efforts to provide clean, caring hospital environments. As the Northern army recognized the need for more help, a few female nurses were allowed to join directly in the care giving. These numbers grew and grew.

The earliest nurses found acceptance difficult. War was a man's world, and it was felt that ladies should not be witnessing such carnage. But the dedication and determination shown by many female nurses did not go unnoticed. They began to be accepted for a variety of duties, from cleaning, to cooking, to writing letters for soldiers. Soon their duties included changing bandages, giving medicine and assisting with procedures. It wasn't long before nurses were in demand, and they, in turn, began demanding more supplies and better conditions for injured soldiers.

Because the battles were mostly fought in enemy held land, the injured Union soldiers often needed to be taken great distances back to Northern hospitals. This lead to redesigning boats and hospital trains outfitted with bunks to carry the injured in some comfort. Nurses staffed these trains and boats, taking pride in their efforts to get the injured to hospitals in the North.

Some nurses became quite famous, like Clara Barton who ventured onto the blazing battlefields risking her own life to help others. Her work began what is now known as the American Red Cross. Mary Ann Bickerdyke began nursing soldiers in Cairo, Illinois. Her demands for cleaner camps and hospitals made her popular with soldiers who called this strong woman Mother Bickerdyke. She traveled with Grant's and Sherman's armies for four years in nineteen battles from Fort Donelson to Atlanta. General Sherman said of her, "She ranks me."

After the Civil War, nursing became a respected profession as women assumed a larger role in the world of care giving.

Patients in Ward K, Armory Hospital, Washington, DC

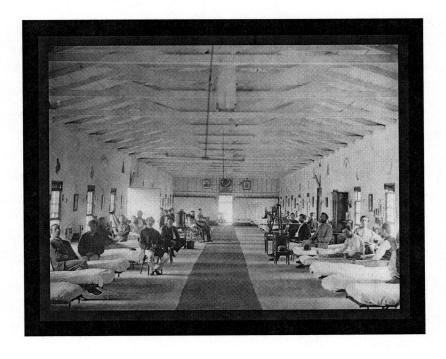

"In this sad world of ours, sorrow comes to all: and, to the young, it comes with bitterest agony, because it takes them unawares."
A. Lincoln December 23, 1862 Letter to Fanny McCullough

Nurses, South

Nurses in the South faced the same dilemma as in the North. Refined young ladies were thought to be too delicate for the sights, sounds and smells of an army hospital. Since most battles were fought in Southern states, it was sometimes quite possible for family members to provide the nursing care needed. Caring for male family members at home was one thing, but caring for male strangers in a hospital setting was considered indelicate.

After the bloody battles of 1862, the number of injured Confederates skyrocketed and living in the city of Richmond was like living in one immense hospital. Churches, hotels, warehouses, barns and private homes were used as make-shift hospitals while the streets were filled with the overflow. The first Confederate nurses were recuperating soldiers who usually preferred battlefields to bedside duty. So it was not long before white women were needed as nurses, and slaves were needed as orderlies and grave diggers.

Nurses worked hard. They cleaned wounds and scrubbed floors; they performed minor surgeries and cooked meals; they gave out medicine and washed bedding and all the while they were expected to smile and be cheerful.

Rising numbers of injured soldiers caused the Confederate Army to establish the largest hospital in the world in Richmond, Virginia and with it the need for female nurses multiplied as well. Phoebe Yates Pember became the matron of the huge Chimborazo Hospital. To encourage women to dare to become nurses, she wrote," In the midst of suffering and death, ...a woman must soar beyond the conventional modesty considered correct under different circumstances."

Southern women served their country well and when it was over, they gained little recognition nor were they included in war memorials. Yet through them, the nursing profession gained respect.

Wounded from the battles of "The Wilderness" getting fresh air on May 20, 1864.

Occupiers, North

*U*nion forces became the occupiers whenever they entered the Confederate States. As secession began, the United States declared that all forts belonged to the Federal government wherever they were located. So when the Confederacy declared Fort Sumter as its own, Southerners viewed Northern ships supplying the fort as aggressors and felt justified to attack the forces on duty. Thus one of the nicknames for the war was The War of Northern Aggression. As Union troops won battles in the South, they took control of the territory and became the occupiers in unfriendly, rebel held land.

Being the occupier had more drawbacks than advantages. First of all, Northerners were in enemy territory and didn't know the lay of the land as well as the enemy did. Getting lost was not an unusual state of affairs as Northern leaders tried to read unfamiliar Southern maps. Plus, Southerners were openly hostile to Union troops and tried to undermine them at every chance.

Northern occupation forces were a long way from home and constantly needed supplies. The army depended on rivers and railroads to transport these supplies of food, arms and provisions which an army of thousands requires. All those miles of railroads were easy targets for guerilla raiders who could disrupt supply lines when and where they pleased. It took thousands of troops to defend these supply trains, troops that were then not available for actual fighting.

The Northern occupiers fared quite well in many of the huge, planned battles throughout the South but they were at a complete disadvantage against the dashing Southern cavalry, especially at the beginning of the war. The Union learned the hard way that it was difficult to fight an enemy whose unpredictable cavalry could gather, attack and vanish before Northern soldiers could retaliate. By 1863, the Federal cavalry began to give as good as it got. A daring brigade of 1,700 raiders, led by Brig. General Benjamin Grierson of Illinois, caused confusion and destruction as they charged through Mississippi on a 600 mile, 16-day raid. This famous foray not only damaged railroads supplying the Southern army at Vicksburg, but it distracted them from the

main attack that General Grant was planning to the South of the city.

There was one advantage, however, to being the occupiers. It was not their own property that was being damaged, nor was it their own land being laid to ruin. Union farms and homes were hundreds of miles away, probably being a bit neglected by their absence, but at least their property was not being destroyed.

"Let your military measures be strong enough to repel
the invader and keep the peace, and not so strong as to
unnecessarily harass and persecute the people."
A. Lincoln May 27, 1863 Letter to John M Schofield

(Photo courtesy of the National Park Service: Fort
Davis National Historic Site, Texas)

Occupied, South

Occupation of one's country by another is seen as a justifiable reason for war. So when the South seceded from the Union and formed their own independent country, they saw themselves as being occupied when the Yankees entered their sovereign lands.

Being the occupied area has many drawbacks. For one thing, the fighting literally takes place in your own towns and farms and backyards. It is your property that is being damaged by the fighting, even if the enemy is being respectful of your hearth and home. Your fields are the ones being trod on, your homes are being used as headquarters and sometimes your food is being eaten. But the advantage of being occupied is that you have a heartfelt desire to protect and defend that which is your own. Being attacked is a great incentive for fighting with all your might.

Southern cavalry raids illustrate the advantage of being occupied. Nathan Bedford Forrest and John Hunt Morgan were cavalry leaders who seemed to know every back road and every hiding place. Plus, they had the support of the people nearby. Commanding small units, they could gather at short notice, stage a fierce raid on Northern troops or supply lines and then just as quickly, fade into the population. These guerillas carried out hit and run operations that destroyed railroad lines and supply depots that were crucial to the Northern soldiers far from home.

The vast majority of the fighting in the Civil War took place in the Southern states, so when they surrendered, not only did the Southerners feel defeated and humiliated, there was also overwhelming destruction to confront. President Lincoln knew the uphill struggle the soldiers would face upon returning home and he therefore ordered no retribution against the Southerners. A generous peace allowed the soldiers to return home with their mules and horses, and officers to keep their weapons. Thus began the long, slow process of healing the nation.

Wilmer McLean's homes were occupied in a most unique way. His home in Manassas, Virginia, was used by the Southern army as headquarters for General P. T. Beauregard during the battle of First Manassas or Bull Run. But when a cannonball crashed into their kitchen, the McLean family decided to move out of the war theater. They moved what they thought was a safe distance away... to Appomattox Courthouse, a town 143 miles away. There, at the end of the war, the Union and Confederate generals met to sign a peace treaty.

"The war started in my front yard and ended in my front parlor."
Wilmer McLean

President Lincoln, North

Lincoln was elected the 16th President of the United States in November of 1860. He said farewell to his home town of Springfield, Illinois, in February 1861 and headed to Washington City, noting that he faced a task "greater than that which rested upon Washington." And so he did.

Just getting to the capital was challenging because already there were threats against his life. Switching trains and sneaking into the city caused the President to be ridiculed by his enemies which caused him to promise never to take such unnecessary precautions again. Throughout his presidency Lincoln freely walked the streets of Washington and rode his horse to the summer White House in the nearby countryside, without guards or fear, although he was shot at, at least once.

The Lincoln family moved into the Executive Mansion after his Inauguration on March 4, 1861. Mary Lincoln spent time decorating the parlors and herself. She had always seen herself as the belle of the ball and this was to be her grandest stage of all. Their eldest son, Robert, spent most of the White House years at Harvard. But the two youngest Lincolns, Willie and Tad, spent their time playing throughout the house and yards with their friends Bud and Holly Taft. The boys were rambunctious, charming and frustrating children who usually got their way. In January of 1862 the boys became ill, probably from drinking contaminated water from the Potomac River. In February, Willie died and suddenly the joyful sounds of children no longer rang through the halls.

President Lincoln spent his time in much the same way every day. An egg for breakfast; meetings with cabinet members; writing letters; waiting in the War Department for battle results to come in on the telegraph; meetings with generals; writing a speech; visiting a battlefield or a hospital; worrying; trying to sleep and then getting up the next day and doing it all over again. In the summer, when the oppressive heat in Washington made everyone wonder why the capital was located where it was, the Lincoln family moved out to the Soldiers' Home for a breath of cooler air. But the stress of being a wartime president took its toll. Abraham Lincoln aged markedly during the war years as his vision of saving the Union expanded to include the freeing of slaves as well.

When Richmond, the capital of the confederacy, finally fell in April 1865, President Lincoln and his son Tad walked into the Confederate White House and Lincoln sat in Jefferson Davis' chair. Only then did the President dare to smile.

"Peace does not appear so distant as it did. I hope it
will come soon, and come to stay; and so come as
to be worth the keeping in all future time."
A. Lincoln August 26, 1863 Letter to James Conkling

ANDERSON BUILDING.

The Lincoln family spent the hot summer months in the Anderson Cottage at the Soldiers' Home just a few miles north of the White House. The President rode his horse back and forth to the White House on a daily basis to carry out the business of the land. He often rode alone, unguarded, with no worries. But after a bullet shot through his hat, he reluctantly agreed to be guarded by soldiers.

President Davis, South

Jefferson Davis was the one and only President of the Confederate States of America. Ironically, he would have preferred to serve his country in the military, but his countrymen elected him their President.

Although Jefferson Davis was born in Kentucky on June 3, 1808, within 100 miles of the birthplace of Abraham Lincoln, their lives took them on remarkably different paths. The Davis family moved south to Louisiana and Mississippi while the Lincoln family headed north and west to Indiana and Illinois. Davis attended years of schooling followed by college before he attended West Point; Lincoln believed all his days of schooling only added up to about one year. Davis was a US Congressman and then a US Senator; and while Jefferson Davis was a Senator, Abraham Lincoln was a young Congressman.

Jefferson Davis owned slaves and was a staunch believer in giving states the right to decide many issues. He believed that the federal government should be kept small so as to avoid becoming a monarchy like the one in England we had rebelled against in 1776. He believed that states should have their own militias, their own roads and rail systems and their own banks and currencies. And certainly they should have the right to decide if they wanted to continue the institution of slavery.

Davis was a tall, dignified man who preferred to make his own decisions and to stand by them without listening to the opinions of others. He was easily insulted and bore grudges. He found it frustrating to get the leaders of the Confederate states to work together, but on the other hand, he continued to insist on their individual state rights. Some say the South died of state's rights.

In the last days of the Confederacy, Jefferson Davis and his cabinet evacuated Richmond on a train loaded with Confederate currency and documents. He was captured by Federals on May 10, 1865, and imprisoned in Fort Monroe, Virginia. He was released on bail two years later.

In his last years, Davis traveled and wrote books on the Confederacy. When he died on December 6, 1889, the South staged a huge farewell as his funeral train traveled from New Orleans to Richmond, Virginia where he was buried with many honors.

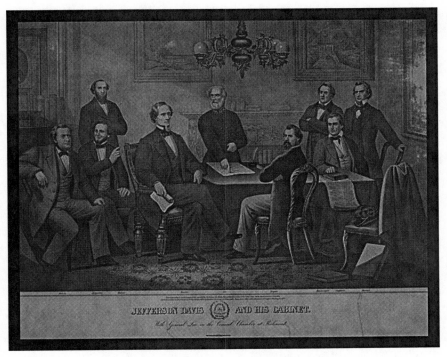

Jefferson Davis and His Cabinet

Quaker Guns, North and South

Quaker guns were fake guns used by both sides during the Civil War to give the impression of superior artillery strength. Since Quakers are a pacifist religious group, which means they do not approve of fighting nor do they participate in wars, giving the "non-gun" the name Quaker Gun is appropriate.

The Southern army perhaps used Quaker Guns more because it was smaller than the Union army and had fewer guns and supplies. While the North had several factories which manufactured weapons, the more rural South had one main factory, the Tredegar Iron Works in Richmond. So to compete against the Union's larger forces and available artillery, the rebels used clever tricks to augment their resources.

In March of 1862, Confederate General Joseph E. Johnston, used Quaker Guns to his advantage at Centerville, Virginia. Rebel soldiers cut down huge trees, cleverly shaping and painting the wood to look like heavy artillery. After they were positioned, the men completed their charade by marching in circles for hours, making it look like thousands of rebel soldiers were ready to do battle with plenty of cannon. They knew that the Northern scouts would erroneously report the Southern strength as much greater than it really was. Union General McClellan hesitated, then declined the chance to engage the much exaggerated Southern forces. After the rebels were long gone, the Northern army was embarrassed to find that Quaker guns were all that stood between them and a sure-fire victory.

Northern troops were also known to employ this technique. Payback is fair play! After the evacuation of Northern troops at a battle near

Harrison's Landing, rebels found not only Quaker guns but abandoned cardboard figures still standing at their posts.

OH NO! Fooled by log cannons and scarecrows!

Pretending to fire a Quaker Gun.

Railroads, North

Railroads were the life blood of the growing nation called the United States of America in the 1800's. In 1850 the Iron Horse ran on 9,000 miles of track. But by 1860 there was an astonishing 30,000 miles of track which was more than the rest of the world combined! Most of these Northern rail lines ran east to west and tied together the destinies of the pioneers with the Northerners who were supplying their every need. The North/South rail lines played a large, supporting role in the Civil War as troops and supplies crisscrossed the countryside.

The North especially depended on railroads as the Union troops fought deep into rebel territory. Some trains carried troops and some carried food, supplies and arms to the men in the field. But don't think of trains as only suppliers of goods. Think of them as fighting machines as well.

For example, a locomotive could be a battering ram if sent flying down the track with a full head of steam to crash intentionally into an enemy train. Or a train car or two could be set on fire directly under a bridge causing not only the destruction of the bridge but also causing confused delays as the enemy army was forced to reroute troops. Heavy guns loaded onto flatbed cars could quickly be moved to new locations on a speeding Iron Horse. These guns could even be fired while the train was moving, a kind of predecessor to today's tanks.

As a tank, a battering ram and a delivery truck, railroads were so valuable that they were themselves objects of attack. Each side knew the weakness of trains covering long, lonely routes. Jobs on trains were nothing if not dangerous. To protect the people and valuable armament on the trains against enemy fire, metal shields were sometimes attached to deflect bullets and cannon balls. The North had to assign many soldiers to protect trains and depots, soldiers who were then not available in battles.

Even the North with its rail superiority found its life lines were in constant need of repairs and rebuilding. The United States Military Railroads' Construction Corps became famous for its engineering feats, quickly and efficiently rebuilding bridges, clearing tunnels and keeping the rail system, and thus the Union army, successful and moving.

The Dictator Gun provided the North with a movable defense system.

Railroads, South

Southern railroads were plagued with issues. First of all, there were not nearly as many rail lines in the South as in the more industrialized North. Second, the lines were sometimes not the same gauge. This meant that a train on one line could travel only so far and then supplies would have to be unloaded and reloaded onto another line, wasting time and valuable manpower. Third, nearly all Southern locomotives and rails were manufactured in the North or in England making replacing them almost impossible during wartime.

So the Southerners spent much of their energy in disrupting the rail lines that the Union was using. It was easy for mounted rebels to destroy rails and bridges and steal valuable Union supplies. Southern soldiers became famous for these hit and run attacks. John Hunt Morgan and Nathan Bedford Forrest were two of several Confederate cavalry officers commanding thousands of guerrilla soldiers as well as regular units. These irregulars had no camps, no supply lines and they left no tracks. They seemingly came out of no where and disappeared into thin air after doing their damage. Union troops could not find them to pursue them. These raiders rode like they had been born on horseback, lived off the land, knew every back road in the area, and had sympathetic supporters on most every farm and country lane. Using prearranged signals, they gathered and swarmed like bees against the Northern aggressors and then they were gone, usually unharmed.

In August of 1862, Morgan's men attacked in middle Tennessee. They successfully blocked Union supply lines by pushing flaming box cars into a huge tunnel, causing the timbers to burn and the tunnel to cave in. This caused huge Union delays and frustration. With only 2,500 men, Forest and Morgan had thwarted an army of 40,000!

As long as the Union army depended on supply lines, these raids were very damaging to Northern progress. It was to take another year before the Northerners learned to travel light and live off the land. By the time Union General William T. Sherman made his famous March to the Sea, his men were pros at living without supply lines.

Both sides enjoyed the sport of tearing up railroad tracks to thwart the progress of supply trains. During General Sherman's March to the Sea, torn up tracks were heated and wrapped around tree trunks, earning them the nickname "Sherman's Neck ties."

Secession, North

Secession means to withdraw from a group and in this case it meant withdrawing from the United States of America. But could states leave the union whenever they wished? President Elect Abraham Lincoln and most Northerners thought not. Lincoln referred to the Declaration of Independence to make his point. In that document the thirteen *Colonies* had been transformed into the United *States*; so, he reasoned, without the United States there would be no individual states, only colonies. Therefore, national power is superior to state rights because it came first. Furthermore, the Constitution gave the federal government sovereignty in the all-important matters of national defense, foreign policy, foreign commerce and coining money.

The Constitution has no provision for states to secede. Therefore, in 1861, President Lincoln swore to preserve, honor and defend the Constitution in the whole country. Thus, Lincoln viewed disunion as illegal, an act which needed to be put down at all costs. For him, the Confederacy was never a separate country.

After Lincoln's election, last minute compromises to avoid Civil War were proposed by Northerners as well as Southerners. Although most wished to avoid violence, Northerners saw these proposed compromises as attempts to bully the Union into agreements that favored the South. For example, in one compromise proposal, the South demanded amendments guaranteeing the right to keep slaves against any future government interference and they insisted that these proposed amendments were to be valid for all time and no *future* amendment could ever override them!

Lincoln would have no part in such compromises. While still in Springfield, he wrote to William Kellogg, "Entertain no proposition for a compromise in regard to the extension of slavery....The tug has to come & better now than later." He sensed that Southern demands once met would never end.

With no compromise, seven states seceded: South Carolina lead the way on December 20 followed by Mississippi, Florida, Alabama, Georgia, Louisiana and Texas. Probably no compromise would have stopped these states in the lower South from seceding as the 1860 election of the "Black Republican", Abraham Lincoln, had triggered their decision and he was not compromising.

THE HERCULES OF THE UNION.
SLAYING THE GREAT DRAGON OF SECESSION.

In this cartoon, General Winfield Scott is Hercules slaying the many-headed dragon of secession. His club says "Liberty and Union". The dragon's neck has seven heads, each representing a Southern leader and their vice.

From the top the heads are:
1) Hatred and Blasphemy, Confederate Secretary Robert Toombs.
2) Lying, Confederate Vice President Alexander Stephens
3) Piracy, President Jefferson Davis
4) Perjury, Commander P.G.T. Beauregard
5) Treason, US General David E. Twiggs, who in February 1861 turned over 19 federal army posts in Texas to the South.
6) Extortion, South Carolina Governor Francis W. Pickens
7) Robbery, Secretary of War John B. Floyd, accused of supplying Federal arms and supplies to the South

"Plainly, the central idea of secession, is the essence of anarchy."
A. Lincoln March 4, 1861 Inaugural Address

Secession, South

Secession looked very different to folks in the South. The Confederates based their argument on the Constitution. Since states existed prior to the Constitution, they believed that state rights took precedence over national rights. Southerners wanted to keep decision making powers close to home, fearing a strong federal government which always seemed to interfere with their rights regarding slavery. Therefore, the South advocated the right of a state to leave the Union at will. More than one state in the South had threatened to secede long before the fateful year of 1860.

For example, Senator John C. Calhoun, from South Carolina, was one of the early supporters of secession. As early as 1828, Calhoun loudly and emphatically suggested that each state should have the right to **nullify** any federal law it deemed undesirable (such as tariffs.) He advocated secession as a better alternative to accepting federal laws with which the South disagreed. For years he and other "fire-eaters" tried hard but could not convince enough South Carolinians that secession was the best alternative.

And so it finally came to pass that soon after Lincoln was elected in 1860, amid huge rallies, marching bands and slogans of state's rights, South Carolina became the first state to secede on December 20, 1860. Considering how few citizens actually owned slaves, "secession-fever" had to convince a lot of non-slave holders that it was a gross violation of *their* rights as well to remain in the Union. Threats of possible future danger to all their wives and daughters if slaves were set free did the trick. Fear is a great unifier and no last minute compromise could stop the roll toward secession and Civil War.

When South Carolina seceded, it declared that all federal forts in the state were by rights now theirs. Several forts fell easily but Fort

Sumter, out in the middle of Charleston's harbor, remained under federal control. With no surrender in sight, South Carolina's artillery fired on Fort Sumter on April 12, 1861. This caused President Lincoln to enforce his sworn duty to protect the United States of America and when he called up federal troops, the South regarded this as a declaration of war. Soon Virginia, Arkansas, North Carolina and Tennessee seceded as well. The stage was set to decide the issue of slavery once and for all.

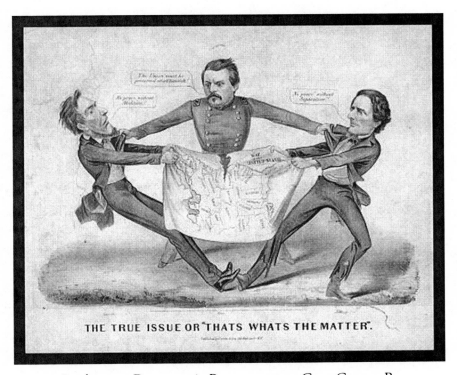

In this pro-Democratic Party cartoon, Gen. George B. McClellan is the go-between in a tug of war over a map of the United States. McClellan says, "The Union must be preserved at all hazards!" Lincoln tugs at the Northern side and says, "No peace without abolition." Davis pulls at the Southern portion saying, "No peace without separation."

Tents, North

*T*ents came in a variety of shapes and sizes, but they were to serve one purpose only...to protect soldiers from rain, snow, sleet and sun wherever the war took them. Some tents were more successful than others.

In his Civil War diary, John M. King, of the 92nd Illinois, describes bell tents as large tents resembling the shape of cow bells. These tents were held up with two poles and a cross bar. The lower edge was then staked to the ground with an opening that could be buttoned at one end.

"The usual mode of sleeping, after littering the ground with straw or hay if it could be had, was to lie with feet towards the center ...and our heads out. We used knapsacks for pillows. In this way, twenty men could be crowded into one tent, provided the boys would "spoon up" just right."

Turning over was a group effort, led by the desire of one man and followed of necessity by the others. Twenty unwashed men shut up all night in a water-tight tent was an unhealthy, not to mention smelly, place to sleep.

These large tents had to be transported by wagons, so when men were marching in the field, a smaller tent was more useful. These were called dog tents, which the men "received with many barks and growls at first." Nowadays these small tents are called "pup" tents. Each man was given his own tent which was small enough to be rolled up and easily carried with the soldier's other necessities. Men could sleep alone in their tent or "two soldiers could button their tent pieces together" making a tent just big enough for sleeping or writing letters home.

During winter months the marching and fighting lessened and

soldiers were able to make a more permanent tent for themselves. They began by digging a one-or-two foot hole in the ground the size of the tent. This made the structure warmer. Notched logs built up the sides like stockade walls. A tent was stretched over the top as a roof. These cozy little homes were furnished with hand made beds and tables and benches, took several days to build and were sometimes lived in for several months before spring announced the arrival of a new fighting season and the need to move on.

Summer quarters, complete with shade, for
Union Officers in Arlington, VA

Winter quarters with log base for extra warmth

Tents, South

Tents in the Confederacy ranged in size from small to non-existent. For though the South was famous for growing top-notch cotton, they were under prepared in manufacturing. Thus, the soldiers were poorly supplied with tents, uniforms and provisions of all kinds.

So it was a joyful day when Southern troops obtained tents as well as other supplies after battles against better supplied Northern troops. Confiscated tents, cooking utensils, shoes and supplies were then gleefully shared by the victorious Southerners. O.T. Hanks wrote in his diary after the battle of Gaines Mill:

"We have had a glorious victory with its rich Booty. A many one of our boys now have a pair of Britches a nice rubber cloth and a pair of blankets also a pair or more of Small Tent Cloths."

Of course, ambushing supply trains and wagons was even better as this provided Southerners with brand new equipment!

Due to often limited provisions, the Confederate soldiers spent many a night tentless with only a blanket or rubber poncho between themselves and the stars.

1st Lt. Montgomery of the 3rd Battalion Georgia Sharpshooters wrote from Lookout Mountain, Tennessee on October 24, 1863,

"We have no tents yet, so we have to make out as best we can by stretching our blankets."

A popular tent in the Rebel army was the Tent-Fly. Tent-Flys were supposed to be an extra covering over the top of a larger tent, essentially giving more protection in times of rain, sleet and snow. Southern troops made good use of them as their sole tent which they found to be much better than sleeping with none at all. And, since the ends were open, there was good ventilation when the tents were crowded with 15 or more men who rarely had access to adequate bathing facilities!

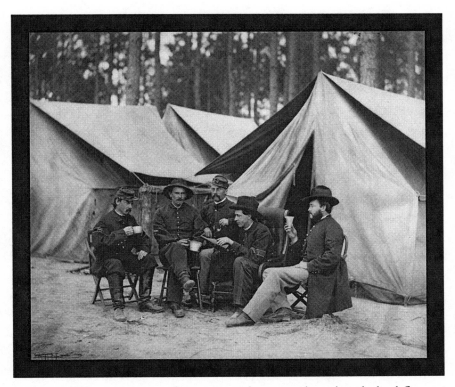

Fly tents were meant to fly over another tent that already had flaps. Northern troops used them for extra protection. Southern troops considered themselves lucky to have any tent at all and often used fly tents as their only protection, not minding the open ends.

Uniforms, North

*U*niforms were anything and everything except uniform at the beginning of the conflict. From the plain clothes brought from home, to the brilliant red Zouave uniforms, to kilts worn by a group of Scots, uniforms were as diverse as the soldiers themselves.

The famous Union Blue uniforms were not readily available at the beginning of the war. This often led to confusion and hesitation when firing weapons, for fear of shooting fellow soldiers. At the first battle of Bull Run, Union troops withheld fire on bluish-clad soldiers in the fight for Henry House Hill, thinking they were reinforcements. Valuable minutes went by before they were discovered to be the 33rd Virginia who proceeded to level their muskets and fire on the Yankees at deadly close range.

Manufacturing uniforms took time that the armies didn't have. In fact, on July 4, 1861, in a message to Congress, President Lincoln remarked that "one of the greatest perplexities of the government, is to avoid receiving troops faster than it can provide for them." Manufacturers hurrying to fill orders for thousands of uniforms simply compressed the fibers of recycled woolen goods instead of weaving them. Known as "shoddy", this fabric disintegrated quickly if worn in rain and tore easily if stretched. To this day, the word shoddy refers to anything made with poor workmanship. Soon, however, the might of the industrialized North kicked into high gear and was able to provide quality uniforms for the troops.

Uniforms consisted of gear as well as clothing. Soldiers carried everything they needed as they marched from campsite to battlefield. John M. King of the 92nd Illinois, described a soldier's uniforms in detail:

"Besides the suit on his back he carried an overcoat, two woolen blankets, a dress coat, a rubber blanket, an extra pair of pants, one extra shirt, portfolio, stationery, and a bottle of ink. All this was placed in a knapsack. In addition he had a haversack to carry rations, cartridge box with belts, forty rounds of cartridge, bayonet scabbard, bayonet, and musket."

By adding other "necessities" such as a coffee pot, frying pan, and dog tent, the typical soldier carried more than 50 pounds of gear while marching mile upon mile in the heat of summer and the cold of winter.

"The causes of the war were wide apart
but the manhood was the same."
Col. Joshua Lawrence Chamberlain, 20th Maine

Uniforms, South

Uniforms in the South were even less uniform than those in the North. Strange as it seems, although the South grew abundant, high-quality cotton for themselves and the world, it did not have the factories to manufacture uniforms and blankets. Woolen uniforms, manufactured in the North, were not available to the South as trading became illegal as soon as the war began. This left Southern soldiers to their own devices when it came to providing cooler, cotton uniforms.

Families typically made their own clothing so it followed that family members sewed up many uniforms as well. Wealthy officers had tailors and/or slaves back home to sew handsome uniforms for themselves. Individual states provided some uniforms, adding much to the variety.

The South preferred Cadet Gray for their uniforms while the North chose Union Blue: hence, the conflict is sometimes called the Blue vs. the Gray.

As the war progressed, the dye needed to make Cadet Gray was no longer available. Substitute dyes produced a color more yellowish than gray and the somewhat derogatory nickname "butternuts" came into being.

West Point officers and Virginia Military Institute cadets donned fancy uniforms with brass buttons and gauntlets. Privates proudly wore plainer uniforms.

"I had on a new Confederate gray suit, with bright Confederate buttons sent to me from home just before I left Camp Chase."

Private William M. Moss, Company D 1st Tennessee, 1865

Vicksburg, North

Vicksburg, Mississippi with its strategic location high on the bluffs overlooking the Mississippi River, was very important to the Union Army because the Confederate Army stationed there controlled passage up and down the mighty river. This prevented Union troop movement on the "Father of Waters" while allowing the rebels much needed access to the western arena of the war (Texas, Louisiana and Arkansas.) If the Union could defeat the rebels at Vicksburg, the Confederacy would be split in two and the war would surely be over soon.

General Grant's first attacks on Vicksburg were easily repulsed by the rebels. So in May of 1863, he opted to try a surprise attack from the south. However, his army was north of the city! To accomplish this, his whole army of 23,000 men would have to march down the western side of the river, cross thirty miles below Vicksburg, and surprise them with an attack from an unexpected direction. Yet, how could so many soldiers march that far unnoticed? There were thousands of men, horses, mules and wagons...how could they NOT be seen or heard?

They would need a diversion. This was accomplished by sending a cavalry force lead by General Benjamin Grierson through the heart of Mississippi, disrupting the railroads, burning warehouses, and fighting in small skirmishes. For sixteen days these fast riding, clever soldiers kept the attention of the Confederate army on themselves while General Grant tiptoed his whole army down the western side past Vicksburg. Thirty miles south, they quickly crossed the river without being noticed. Now they were close enough to attack by land. Yet, each attack was repulsed by thousands of deeply entrenched Confederates proving that "one soldier under cover was the equal of at least three in the open."

If victory could not be had in battle, Grant reasoned, he would win by starving them out. Thus began the siege of Vicksburg which lasted about six weeks. Union troops encircled the city, keeping out food supplies and aid. Confederate soldiers and citizens tried their best to keep up their spirits in the face of constant bombardments which prevented sleep while destroying their city. As well, Union soldiers repeatedly tunneled under enemy trenches and set off explosions that further disoriented the southern troops. Finally, malnourished, exhausted and downhearted, 30,000 rebel soldiers surrendered on the Fourth of July, 1863.

The Siege of Vicksburg

At the very same time, the Battle of Gettysburg was won by the Union. Thus the Southern army was thwarted in the east and in the west. Although the war would not be over for one and a half more years, General Grant said,

"the fate of the Confederacy was sealed when Vicksburg fell."

Vicksburg, South

Vicksburg seemed to have it all. It was a prosperous city, safely perched atop a high bluff strategically overlooking the Mighty Mississippi River, a center of business and wealth. With such a commanding view and physical control over river traffic, people nicknamed it "the Gibraltar of the West." By 1863, the Confederacy had lost many battles and was weakening. It desperately needed to keep control of the Mississippi River for shipping supplies, armaments and personnel. With the fall of New Orleans to the Union forces in 1862, Vicksburg was the South's last hope to keep the Confederacy united.

The defenders of Vicksburg successfully repelled General Grant's first attempt to defeat them via water in the spring of 1863. From their lofty vantage point 200 feet above the river, the Confederate army launched heavy cannon balls which rained down on Union ships as they tried to steam past Vicksburg to get close enough to attack. The citizens of Vicksburg seemed well fortified on the river side, and well defended on the land side by their own troops and thousands of reinforcements not far away. They did not know that their advantageous position would soon be to their disadvantage.

When General Grant's forces surprised the city and attacked instead by land, no aid could reach the isolated rebels. The surrounded citizens were certain that they could outlast the Union troops. So they hunkered down for a long siege. Intent on withstanding the 24 hour a day bombardment by the Union forces, the worn down citizens and the Confederate army alike lived in caves and trenches while their homes and beautiful city were destroyed. When food supplies ran low, they ate what they could including rats, cats and dogs, believing that if they could just hold out a little longer, reinforcements would certainly arrive. To the very end, the Vicksburg newspaper, down to one square foot printed on wall paper, encouraged, "Hold out a few days longer, and our lines will be opened , the enemy driven away, the siege raised."

Finally, starving and sleep deprived, the proud citizens of Vicksburg admitted to themselves that no help was coming to their rescue.

Thirty thousand Confederate troops under General Pemberton surrendered on the saddest Fourth of July the devastated city would ever know; and one which they would never forget.

During the siege and shelling of Vicksburg, citizens lived in cave-like dug outs earning the nickname, "Prairie Dog" town.

West Point, North

West Point Military Academy was founded in 1802 on the banks of the Hudson River in New York. To become a cadet at such a prestigious school, one must be nominated by a member of Congress and face rigid entrance requirements. Many future Union Civil War officers, including Generals Ulysses S. Grant, William Tecumseh Sherman, George McClellan and George Custer, graduated from West Point. They studied engineering as well as military tactics and were involved in some of the biggest engineering projects of the time, such as rerouting the Mississippi River to keep it flowing near the city of St. Louis.

The spirit of West Point affected these men the rest of their lives. In the deep friendships made there, the young men felt a sense of comradeship and a sense of belonging to something important. This loyalty to each other was even felt on the opposing battlefields during the Civil War.

West Point suffered resignations of cadets when Southern states began seceding prior to the start of the Civil War. All in all, over three hundred cadets and graduates defected in the spring of 1861, raising criticism and doubts in the North over the teachings of the academy which could produce so many traitors. This backlash by influential Northerners against West Pointers caused Lincoln to hesitate in appointing graduates to high ranking positions in the army. Hence, the North struggled to find strong military leaders which might in part explain why the Union got off to a poor start in the war.

When these old West Point friends met next on battlefields, interesting exchanges occurred. In 1862, when General Ulysses S. Grant defeated Brigadier General Simon Buckner at Fort Donelson, Tennessee, Grant handed his own purse to his fellow West Pointer in case Buckner needed money. (Think of this also as fair play: Buckner had lent Grant money when Grant needed money to get home when he resigned from the army in 1854!)

The day the South surrendered at Appomattox, the McLean House was filled with West Pointers on both sides. Perhaps deep friendships influenced the easy terms of the surrender advocated by President Lincoln. Allowing the defeated Southern army to freely return home unpunished was surprising in itself. But allowing officers to keep their side arms and soldiers to keep their horses, made for the possibility of a successful peace.

The Plain at West Point
(Courtesy of Lou Hester)

West Point, South

West Point's motto, DUTY, HONOR and COUNTRY became a problem for Southern cadets and graduates as their consciences were tested in 1861. They felt a deep loyalty to the United States if the crisis involved a foreign country, such as during the Mexican War in 1846. But when the crisis involved their own states, an even stronger loyalty was felt. Thus, as the Civil War began, many cadets and graduates chose to be loyal to their state rather than to their country.

The firing on Fort Sumter in April 1861 caused the rules at West Point to be changed to reflect this new threat to the United States. In the past, cadets had been asked to swear an oath of allegiance as citizens of individual states. Now they were being asked to swear allegiance to the United States itself. Ten cadets refused to take the new oath and were immediately dismissed. In all, over three hundred cadets and graduates resigned their commissions and many were immediately appointed high positions in the Confederate Army.

The most famous resignation was by Robert E. Lee who had graduated West Point in 1829 with high praise and NO demerits. He had been Superintendent of the Academy during the 1850's and was President Lincoln's first choice to take charge of the Union forces. However, Lee's loyalty to his home state of Virginia won out and the Confederacy benefited from his talents and expertise during and even after the Civil War.

Jefferson Davis, Class of 1828, became the President of the Confederacy. Stonewall Jackson, P.T. Beauregard, and George Pickett became famous Confederate generals who showed that they had learned their West Point lessons on military tactics very well. For example, in the Shenandoah Valley campaign in 1862, General Stonewall Jackson skillfully demonstrated his tactical expertise by quickly and boldly moving his heavily outnumbered troops to successfully prevent General McClellan from getting reinforcements.

Of the sixty major battles in the Civil War, fifty-five were commanded on both sides by West Point graduates.

West Point Generals in Civil War
This is a partial list of the nearly 450 West Point graduates who were generals during the Civil War.

Union Generals
Anderson, Robert, 1825
Buell, Don Carlos, 1841
Buford, John, 1848
Burnside, Ambrose Everett, 1847
Custer, George Armstrong, 1861
Doubleday, Abner, 1842
Grant, Ulysses Simpson, 1843
Halleck, Henry Wagner, 1839
Hooker, Joseph, 1837
King, Rufus, 1833
McClellan, George Brinton, 1846
Meade, George Gordon, 1835
Ord, Edward Otho Cresap, 1839
Pope, John, 1842
Rosecrans, William Starke, 1842
Sheridan, Philip Henry, 1853
Sherman, William Tecumsah, 1840

Confederate Generals
Beauregard, Pierre Gustave T. 1838
Bragg, Braxton, 1837
Early, Jubal Anderson 1837
Ewell, Richard Stoddert, 1840
Helm, Benjamin Hardin, 1851
Hood, John Bell, 1853
Jackson, Thomas J. "Stonewall", 1846
Johnston, Albert Sidney, 1826
Johnston, Joseph Eggleston, 1829
Lee, Fitzhugh, 1856
Lee, George Washington Custis, 1854
Lee, Robert Edward, 1829
Longstreet, James, 1842
Magruder, John Bankhead, 1830
Pemberton, John Clifford, 1837
Pickett, George Edward, 1846
Stuart, James Ewell Brown, 1854

eXchange of Prisoners, North

eXchanging prisoners of war did not formally begin with the first battles of the Civil War. In fact, when the War Between the States began, both sides seemed unprepared to transport and care for their prisoners. So informal eXchanges of prisoners occurred as small, early battles ended and close proximity allowed. Swapping prisoners was as easy as crisscrossing a brook with equal numbers of soldiers being traded. But as the war went on and the numbers of prisoners increased, trading became impossible. Prisoners were haphazardly housed in a motley assortment of run down buildings, factories and even barns. Some were sent to army camps, as in the case of Camp Douglas, Chicago, where over 4,000 rebels were sent after the battle of Fort Donelson, Tennessee, in February, 1862. The camp was not equipped to house so many, and the southern prisoners suffered from cold winds off Lake Michigan and filthy sewage conditions due to swampy surroundings. Underclothed and underfed, one out of eight prisoners died of exposure and illness during their six month stay.

Both North and South agreed that something had to be done, and an organized system of eXchange was developed wherein soldiers could be traded by rank. For example, a non-commissioned officer could be traded for two privates, a lieutenant could be traded for four privates, and so on up until a general could be traded for sixty privates. By September the Confederate prisoners at Camp Douglas were all formally eXchanged for Union prisoners, and the unhealthy POW camp on Chicago's lakefront was empty for a short while.

But by 1863 a new problem stopped the eXchanges. The Union army by then had enlisted many black soldiers (freedmen and former slaves), but the Confederate army refused to eXchange any captured black soldiers, preferring to shoot them or return them to their former owners.

Lincoln insisted that eXchanges be color-blind. So with eXchanges at a stalemate, the prisons filled up at an alarming rate. After the battle of Vicksburg, Ulysses S. Grant faced the dilemma of what to do with 30,000 POWs and no place to send them. His solution? Parole them. This meant that they were sent home "on their honor" not to fight for the Confederacy until they were formally "eXchanged" at a later date. Grant believed the prisoners could be trusted to keep their word because of the soldier's code of chivalry. He was surprised, disappointed and angry when he recaptured the very same paroled rebels soon after at the battle of Chattanooga.

An artist compares the treatment of Union prisoners
at Andersonville with treatment of Jefferson Davis
while prisoner at Fort Monroe after the war.

eXchange of Prisoners, South

Xchanging prisoners was a dilemma from the Southern point of view as well. The South wanted to exchange Union prisoners for Confederate soldiers as they were desperate to refill their dwindling armies. The sticking point was the black Union soldiers who had been captured. The South would not exchange Negroes because they did not consider them men; to Southerners blacks were still property to be kept in bondage. The North, especially President Lincoln, would not exchange any prisoners unless blacks were included man for man. So thousands of POW's suffered in inadequate prisons in both the North and South.

It is true that in the South, Union prisoners did not face the extreme cold as their Southern counterparts did in the North; but the Northern camps all had buildings or at the least, tents. In the South, prisoners faced the blazing heat of summer in camps where they were provided no protection from the baking sun. In the infamous Andersonville prison in southwestern Georgia, 100 prisoners were dying every day in the summer of 1864 from heat that was as deadly as cold because diseases spread without mercy under such conditions.

Additionally, in 1864-1865, the entire South was facing starvation and inevitably, the Union prisoners were starving equally if not worse than the rest of the population. Eventually, 29% of prisoners in Andersonville died of exposure, disease or malnutrition.

Finally, in March of 1865, the Confederacy was so desperate for manpower that they considered "allowing" their black slaves to fight in the Southern army. Virginia actually passed a bill forming two companies of black soldiers.

This dire necessity also encouraged the South to agree to eXchange "all" prisoners, black and white, but only a few thousand were eXchanged before the peace at Appomattox finally liberated everyone.

Three Confederate Prisoners retain their pride
after the Battle of Gettysburg.

Yankee, North

Yankee referred to Union soldiers during the Civil War. Nowadays it refers to anyone living in the United States. But where did this word come from?

Answer: It began as a way for the colonial English people in America to tease the newly arriving Dutch people who liked to make and eat cheese. Lumping the immigrants together as cheese-eating foreigners, the term John Cheese was pronounced Dutch-like and it came out Yan Kees The derogatory nickname became so prevalent in New England that the British soldiers sang the tune "Yankee Doodle" to ridicule all the poorly dressed colonial soldiers in the Revolutionary War.

By the time of the Civil War a Northern soldier was commonly known as a Yankee or Billy Yank. But the Southern soldiers, proud of their rebellion, called themselves Johnny Rebs. These soldiers had a lot more in common than in difference. Both armies were filled with young men eager for a first taste of glory. Both armies fought battles of illness, poor food, supply shortages, injury and death. Both armies fought mind-numbing boredom interspersed with long marches. "Hurry up and wait" was standard procedure. And, of course, both armies faced the same adrenalin-laced moments of sheer terror during battles.

Ask soldiers from either side why they were fighting, and the answer was curiously similar: "We are fighting for our rights." Of course, the Rebels added, "We are fighting the aggressors from the North" and the Yankees added, "We are fighting for the Union." For most young soldiers the issue of slavery, for or against, was not the reason for enlisting.

Yankees or Yanks became a term of pride in World War I and a popular marching song called *Over There* reassured European nations that the Yankees from <u>anywhere</u> in the USA were coming to help in their defense:

Over there, over there,
*   Send the word, send the word over there*
That the Yanks are coming, the Yanks are coming,
*   The drum's rum-tumming everywhere!*
So prepare, say a prayer,
*   Send the word, send the word to beware*
We'll be over, we're coming over,
*   And we won't come back till it's over, over there!*

Christmas dinner on picket duty was lonely
whether one was a Yankee or a Rebel.

Outskirts of Baltimore
My dear William,
I can now march 20 and 25 miles a day, live on short rations of hard
tack, raw, rancid bacon, green roasting ears and cold water, sleep out in
the rain and heavy dew with nothing but an army coat over me, and enjoy
myself capitally.

Edward Hastings Ripley, 9th Vermont Volunteer Infantry

Johnny Reb, South

Johnny Reb was a proud, young, mostly illiterate Confederate soldier. He typically came from the lower classes of Southerners who did not own slaves. Wealthy Southerners were officers or they chose to purchase a substitute to take their place in the army. This led to the feeling that it was "a rich man's war and a poor man's fight." Many Yankees shared this exact same feeling.

So if Johnny Reb wasn't fighting for slavery, then what motivated him to join up? First and foremost, Johnny Reb fought to protect his homeland from the invading Yankees. He fought so as to appear brave in the eyes of his family and sweetheart. He fought for adventure. He fought for his fellow soldiers and when he attacked the enemy, shrieking the Rebel yell as loudly as he could, he shared a comradery felt by soldiers throughout the ages.

Johnny Reb spent 99% of his time being bored and 1% of his time being terrified. Camp life was dirty and baths were rare, especially in the winter. The food was poor and sickness was rampant. Twice as many soldiers died of illness as died of wounds. Traveling by railroad was a luxury rarely enjoyed by the Southern army which usually traveled on foot. New boots were a scarce commodity so when a pair wore out, it was not unusual to march barefoot.

During battle, life changed markedly. Soldiers recall the terrible noise of gunfire and the chaos that often ensued; the charge into enemy fire; the torture of being hit; and the pain of watching a comrade die.

While in camp, there might be drills lasting most of the day. Chores included digging latrines, collecting firewood and hauling water. But evening always came and with it time to play cards, sing favorite songs and dream of home.

At Stones River, Tennessee on December 30, 1862, the two opposing armies were camped close together preparing for battle the next day. Southern musicians played Dixie and the Bonnie Blue Flag. Northern musicians answered across No-Man's-Land with Yankee Doodle and Hail, Columbia. Then someone began playing Home Sweet Home. Both bands played as one, and soon the armies who would be killing each other the next day joined their voices together in the words they all knew so well.

Confederate Camp, 1864

New Orleans, Louisiana, 1861
I feel that I would like to shoot a Yankee and yet I know that this would not be in harmony with the spirit of Christianity.
William Nugent

Zouaves, North and South

Zouave refers to the style of clothing adopted by French troops in the North African army of Napoleon III. The Algerian soldiers in these French infantry units were famous for their brightly colored uniforms, fancy drills, and military excellence. During the Crimean War in the 1850's, the Zouaves were noticed by military observers from the United States, who brought home tales of their skill and style.

The "Zouave Craze" spread throughout the land through the efforts of Elmer Ellsworth, who transformed a lackluster Chicago militia outfit into the "United States Zouave Cadets." Ellsworth was an ideal drill master after studying the intricacies of French light infantry drill. By 1860 they were known as the finest militia unit in the Midwest. Then Ellsworth challenged other states to compete against them in drills. Their 6-week tour in 1860 awed thousands of spectators who came to watch the exhibitions. Almost immediately dozens of Zouave companies sprang into existence. The New York Times said,

"Their bronzed features, sharp outlines, light, wiry forms, muscular developments and spirited, active movements give them an appearance of dashing ferocity."

When the Civil War began, the government was unable to supply every soldier with standard issue clothing. So some regiments styled their own uniforms after Zouave regiments. The exotic attire came in many forms, but most had a short jacket that did not close in the front, baggy red or blue trousers, white gaiters and a brilliant red, tasseled hat called a fez.

Regiments in both the North and the South adopted these Zouave uniforms and believed that these smart-looking uniforms boosted morale and confidence. Many units became famous for being strong, dependable fighters.

But at times the uniforms were too conspicuous. Bright red is not exactly good camouflage! So there were some who wore standard-issue uniforms in battles and Zouave uniforms for drilling.

DEATH OF COL. ELLSWORTH,

Col. Elmer Ellsworth was the first famous casualty of the Civil War. He was killed bringing down the Confederate flag which was flying at the Marshall House in Alexandria, Virginia. Ellsworth had become a personal friend of Abraham Lincoln and his family after studying law with him in Springfield. President Lincoln was deeply saddened by his friend's death and had his body lie in state in the East Room on May 24, 1861.

"In the untimely loss of your noble son, our affliction here is scarcely less than your own. So much of promised usefulness to one's country, and of bright hopes for one's self and friends, have rarely been so suddenly dashed, as in his fall."

A. Lincoln May 25, 1861 Letter to Ephraim and Phoebe Ellsworth

And then what happened?

The war ended, President Abraham Lincoln was
assassinated, the slaves were freed and all the soldiers
returned home. Peace and brotherhood filled the land
and they all lived happily ever after. Right?

Not quite.

Lincoln's dream for a reunited country lead by our "better
angels" did not easily materialize. A period called Reconstruction
followed the Civil War. It lasted about ten years.

Bad feelings continued to exist between the North
and the South, and between blacks and whites.

Struggles for equal rights continued until the 1960's
and in some ways, they are still going on today.

Yet, to this day, good people of all shades of color
have joined President Lincoln believing in the
essential goodness of the common man.

Reconstruction, North

Reconstruction in the North meant that federal help was needed if the South was going to once again be a contributing partner in the United States of America. Union soldiers were needed to defend black rights; teachers were needed if education for all was to be a priority; and economic help was needed as the South awoke from its four-year nightmare to devastation and poverty.

And so it was that Northerners volunteered to work in the South for about ten years after the merciful peace at Appomattox allowed the Confederate soldiers to simply return home and pick up where they left off. There were no mass imprisonings of Confederate leaders and no mass hangings; instead, Lincoln hoped that the "better angels" of all Americans would come together and lead the country toward liberty and justice for all.

Of course, some took advantage of the situation and tried to make money off the already poor. Northerners and Southerners alike were guilty of lying and cheating to enrich themselves. This is not new in the history of mankind.

When Reconstruction ended, Northerners seemed relieved to have this unpleasant era over with. They were only too ready to focus on their own financial and social problems brought on by a depression in 1873, the Industrial Revolution and Westward Expansion. Issues of Women's Voting Rights and Worker's Rights for better wages and better working conditions in factories kept Northern attention distracted from the plight of freed slaves who found themselves living a new kind of slavery of racial violence and loss of rights.

Yet, blacks persevered with little or no outside help. Through education, hard work and family support, the generations that followed upon generations eventually restored universal civil rights to the grandchildren and great grandchildren of some of the first under-appreciated citizens of the United States of America.

Reconstruction, South

Reconstruction after the Civil War was a huge undertaking, trying to rebuild the entire South physically, socially, economically and legally in just a few short years. In some ways, it succeeded. After the generous peace in 1865, Union troops remained in the South to keep order and to assure freed blacks of their new rights. Many ex-slaves were reunited with family members who had been sold far and wide during the antebellum years. Freed men and women established their own black churches. They voted and ran for office. The Freedman's Bureau had great success in establishing schools for black children while making free elementary education available to poor white children as well.

But try as it might, the Bureau failed to establish goodwill between blacks and whites, and when Reconstruction ended and the military presence returned North, too many of the Southern white population tried to restore their "superiority" by force and fraud. By the 1870's, blacks attempting to vote were being terrorized by the Ku Klux Klan and even by state militias. With little money at hand, blacks were not able to buy land and the government's promise of "40 acres and a mule" never came to be. So ex-slaves all too often found themselves working on plantations and in mines under conditions that were little better than slavery. Yes, even brutal beatings of workers was legal in the new South.

By the 1890's, new state constitutions were written giving whites absolute control. In 1898, Louisiana's Governor Murphy Foster said, "The white supremacy for which we have so long struggled.....is now crystallized into the (state) constitution." So many black elected officials were defeated that in 1901, when Republican Congressman George White from North Carolina left office, he said, "This, Mr. Chairman, is perhaps the Negro's temporary farewell to the American Congress; but let me say that, Phoenix-like, he will rise up and come again."

Despite the violence and loss of rights, the Lincoln legacy of fairness and hope lived on. Brave people of all shades of color made protests and brought lawsuits seeking freedom and justice for all. A hundred years later, in the 1960's, new civil rights legislation made into law their dreams of life, liberty and the pursuit of happiness. Little wonder that in 2008,when Barack Obama was elected the first black President of the United States, hope-filled people of all races believed that Lincoln's "better angels" had succeeded in keeping alive "the last best hope on earth."

Life in Washington City

Washington City became the capital of the United States when Virginia and Maryland donated land to form the District of Columbia. Broad avenues and elegant buildings were designed to give the city the prestige due the capital of the young United States of America.

During the Civil War Washington gave every appearance of being a war city. Soldiers tented on the grounds of the White House; buildings were transformed into hospitals and prisons; ladies rolled bandages and held Sanitary Fairs to support the troops; and like distant thunder, cannons could be heard nearby as the city itself was threatened more than once by advancing Confederate troops. The city became a refuge for newly liberated slaves who fled to Father Abraham and the city that to them represented freedom. They overwhelmed the housing and job markets and often found themselves living in poverty in tent cities.

But in other ways, life in the capital city went on normally. President Lincoln walked worry free through the streets, sometimes visiting Mr. Stuntz's Toy Shop on New York Avenue with Willie and Tad to increase their collection of carved soldiers. Mrs. Lincoln took carriage rides and went shopping. People flocked to Mr. Smithson's recently finished castle full of natural oddities known as the Smithsonian Museum. Folks watched as the dome on the capitol building rose to its completion, and wondered if the monument to President George Washington, halted for lack of funds at 155 feet high, would ever reach its goal of 555 feet. The Willard Hotel offered genteel accommodations and elegant dinners to those who could afford such pleasures. Local theaters still offered nightly plays and Shakespearean dramas which gave the President a few hours blessed relief from the worries of war. And, of course, the first floor of the White House was always open to citizens who sought to speak with the President or to ask a favor of him!

In March of 1865, with the war winding down, one could also see two interesting people on the streets of Washington. One was a teenaged girl who walked to the White House every day at noon while the President took a brief rest at his desk. This talented artist was Vinnie Ream, and she was allowed to work for half an hour each day on a sculpture of the man she most admired. She silently studied his face while working the clay, and her time flew by. Then she covered the bust with a wet towel and tiptoed away. In the evenings she sang for the soldiers in the army hospitals.

The other person was a famous, handsome actor who could be seen wearing a stylish overcoat with distinctive red satin lining under its cape.

No longer interested in practicing his lines and wooing the ladies, he now seemed more interested in studying the alley behind Ford's Theater and the doors leading into the box seats. His name was John Wilkes Booth, renowned for his eloquence, swagger and vigor when acting out violent scenes. His heroes, on stage and off, were the assassins who killed mighty dictators, thus saving their countries from tyranny. He saw himself as the biggest hero of all when he assassinated the "tyrant", Abraham Lincoln. He was unpleasantly surprised when he was met with no cheers or applause from the appalled, heartbroken citizenry.

In the spring of 1865, the statue "Freedom" atop the finally completed capitol dome witnessed two remarkable events: the unbearably sad funeral cortege of President Lincoln, and the unbearably joyful two-day parade of Union soldiers celebrating the end of the long Civil War. If life were fair, their order would have been reversed and Lincoln would have lived to see the momentous parade which included black and white United States soldiers marching side by side at last.

Time Line of Civil War

1619	Slaves sold in Virginia
1808	Importation of slaves outlawed
1820	Missouri Compromise, limiting slavery's expansion
1854	Kansas-Nebraska Act, reversed the Missouri Compromise and allowed states to decide on slavery individually, possibly opening the western territories to slavery
1859	John Brown raided Harpers Ferry
1860	
November 6	Abraham Lincoln elected President of the United States
December 20	South Carolina seceded from the Union
1861	
January 9	Mississippi seceded
January 10	Florida seceded
January 11	Alabama seceded
January 19	Georgia seceded
January 26	Louisiana seceded
February 1	Texas seceded
February 4	Seceded states held a convention in Montgomery, Alabama
February 18	Jefferson Davis inaugurated President of the provisional government of the Confederacy. Alexander Stephens, Vice President, says,

"Our new government ... rests upon the great truth that the Negro is not equal to the white man. This ... government is the first in the history of the world, based on this great physical and moral truth."

March 4	Abraham Lincoln inaugurated as the 16th President of the United States

April 12	Confederates fired on Fort Sumter. Major Robert Anderson lowered the US flag and saved it.
April 15	Lincoln called for states to supply troops
April 17	Virginia seceded
April 18	Robert E. Lee received the offer of Union command (rejected)
April 23	Lee accepted the appointment as commander in chief of Virginia's military forces
May 6	Arkansas seceded
May 20	North Carolina seceded
July 21	Battle of Bull Run (First Manassas) Southern victory
1862	
February 6	Battle of Fort Henry, TN Northern victory
February 12	Battle of Fort Donelson, TN Northern victory
February 22	Jefferson Davis inaugurated President of the Permanent Confederate government in Richmond, Virginia
March 9	Battle of iron clads (*Monitor* vs. CSS *Virginia*)
March 17-July	General McClellan's troops began Peninsula Campaign

Professor Thaddeus S. Lowe's hot air balloon rose above the battlefield to scout the enemy here at Fair Oaks, Virginia (Seven Pines)

March 28   Battle of Glorieta, New Mexico Territory.
             "The Gettysburg of the West" – Union victory

The sign says, "The decisive battle of the Civil War in New
Mexico was fought on this summit, Glorieta Pass, March 28,
1862. Union troops won the battle when a party of Colorado
volunteers burned the Confederate supply wagons, thus
destroying Southern hopes for taking over New Mexico."
(Author's collection)

April 6-7   Battle of Shiloh, Tennessee, Northern victory
April 25   Officer David Farragut took command of New
               Orleans
June 1   Command of Army of Northern Virginia fell to
               Robert E. Lee upon the wounding of General Joseph
               E. Johnston
June 25-July 1 Seven Days' Battles
August 28-30   Union General John Pope defeated at Bull Run
               (Second Manassas)
September 15   Harper's Ferry fell to General Jackson

September 17   Battle of Antietam: 2108 Union soldiers killed, 9549 wounded, 2700 Confederates killed, 9029 wounded. No clear winner, but since Lee withdrew to Virginia, McClellan took credit. This victory allowed President Lincoln to announce the Emancipation Proclamation.

"We could see the deep sadness in the President's face and feel the burden on his heart, thinking of his great commission to save this people and knowing that he could do this no otherwise than as he had been doing – by and through the manliness of these men."
Col. Joshua Lawrence Chamberlain, 20th Maine after the
loss of thousands of men at the Battle of Antietam.

September 22   Lincoln announces his Preliminary Emancipation Proclamation freeing slaves in areas of rebellion as of January 1, 1863
December 13   Battle of Fredericksburg, Confederate win
1863
January 1   Lincoln formally signed the Emancipation Proclamation

January 19-22	Mud March by Army of Potomac
March 3	First Conscription Act. This draft was seen as unfair to the poor and caused riots to erupt in New York City.
April 17	Grierson's Raid begins in Mississippi
May 2-3	Battle of Chancellorsville, Southern victory
May 18-July 4	Siege of Vicksburg, Mississippi begins
July 1-3	Battle of Gettysburg, Pennsylvania, Union victory
July 4	Vicksburg fell to Union troops
August 17	Fort Sumter bombarded by Union
Sept. 19-20	Battle of Chickamauga, Southern victory
November 19	Lincoln dedicated national cemetery with Gettysburg Address
Nov. 23-25	Battle of Chattanooga, Union victory

1864

March 12	Red River Campaign began in Louisiana
April 12	Fort Pillow Massacre
May 5-6	First Battle of the Wilderness near Chancellorsville, VA
May 8-12	Battle of Spotsylvania
June 1-3	Battle of Cold Harbor
July 30	Battle of the Crater, Petersburg, Virginia
September 2	General William T. Sherman's army occupied Atlanta, GA
November	President Lincoln re-elected to second term
Nov. 16-22	Sherman's March through Georgia, ending in Savannah

1865

March 4	Lincoln's Second Inaugural
April 2-3	Union troops occupied Richmond and Petersburg, Virginia
April 9	Lee surrendered at Appomattox Courthouse
April 13	Sherman's March to the Sea ends in Raleigh, NC
April 14	Major Robert Anderson once again raised the US flag over Fort Sumter
April 14	President Lincoln assassinated at Ford's Theater
April 15	Lincoln died, 7:22 am.
April 26	John Wilkes Booth shot and killed in barn in Virginia Johnston surrenders in North Carolina

| May 1 | Lincoln's funeral in Chicago |

May 4	Lincoln with son, William, interred in Springfield, Illinois
	General Taylor surrendered in Alabama
May 10	Jefferson Davis captured in Georgia and began a two-year imprisonment in Fort Monroe
May 22	Mary Lincoln, with sons Robert and Tad, left the White House
May 23-24	Union victory parade down Pennsylvania Avenue in Washington

| May 26 | Smith surrendered in Trans-Mississippi |

July 7   John Wilkes Booth's conspirators hanged in Washington, DC

Mary Surratt, Lewis Powell, David Herald and George Atzerodt

November 6   CSS *Shenandoah* surrendered to British in Liverpool, England

November 10   Henry Wirz hanged for war crimes at Andersonville Prison

December 6   Congress adopted 13th Amendment abolishing slavery

December 13   Ku Klux Klan organized in Pulaski, Tennessee; Confederate General Nathan Bedford Forrest was the First Grand Wizard of the Klan

Time Line of Abraham Lincoln

February 12, 1809
Abraham Lincoln was born about three miles south of Hodgenville, Kentucky. In his short autobiography he wrote, "I was born Feb.12, 1809 in then Hardin County Kentucky."

1811
The Lincoln family moved to Knob Creek.

1816
The Lincoln family moved to Spencer County, Indiana.

October 5, 1818
Nancy Hanks Lincoln, Abraham's mother, died of milk sickness.

December 2, 1819
Thomas Lincoln married Mrs. Sarah Bush Johnston.

January 20, 1828
Lincoln's sister Sarah died in childbirth.

March 15, 1830
The Lincoln family relocated ten miles southwest of Decatur, Illinois

April-July 1831
Lincoln piloted a flat boat to New Orleans and returned to New Salem, Illinois

September 1831
Lincoln began clerking in Denton Offutt's store in New Salem

April 1832
New Salem men volunteered for Black Hawk War and elected Lincoln their captain.

August 6, 1832
Lincoln is defeated in his first bid for the Illinois legislature.

January 15, 1833
Lincoln and William F. Berry purchased a store in New Salem.

May 7, 1833
President Jackson appointed Lincoln postmaster of New Salem.

August 4, 1834
In his second try, Lincoln is elected to the Illinois House of Representatives.

August 25, 1835
Ann Rutledge, close friend of Lincoln, died at the Rutledge farm seven miles northwest of New Salem.

August 1, 1836
Lincoln elected a second time to the Illinois legislature.

September 9, 1836
Lincoln received license to practice law in all courts of the State.

February 24, 1837
The bill to remove the capital of Illinois from Vandalia to Springfield, which Lincoln has promoted, passed the House of Representatives. It passed the Senate on the 25th.

April 15, 1837
Lincoln moved to Springfield at the midpoint of his life. He became the law partner to John Todd Stuart and roomed with Joshua Speed.

August 6, 1838
Lincoln elected to state legislature for the third time.

September 23, 1839
Lincoln became a Circuit Rider in the Eighth Judicial Circuit.

December 9, 1839
The Illinois Legislature met in Springfield for the first time.

August 3, 1840
Lincoln is elected to his fourth term in the Illinois legislature.

January 1, 1841
An emotional crisis upset Lincoln's relations with Mary Todd and he was absent from the legislature for several days.

April 14, 1841
Stuart and Lincoln ended their law partnership and Lincoln became partner with Stephen T. Logan

September 22, 1842
A proposed duel between Lincoln and James Shields was averted when friends talked them out of it.

November 4, 1842
Lincoln and Mary Todd were married at the home of her sister, Elizabeth Todd Edwards, on 2nd Street, in Springfield

August 1, 1843
Robert Todd Lincoln was born to Abraham and Mary while they were living in the Globe Tavern

January 16, 1844
Lincoln purchased a home from Rev. Charles Dresser for $1,200. The Lincoln family moved in on May 1.

December 9, 1844
William H. Herndon was admitted to the bar and the firm Lincoln and Herndon is established.

March 10, 1846
The Lincoln's second child was born and named Edward Baker Lincoln.

December 6, 1847
Lincoln took his seat as a member of the Thirtieth Congress.

March 10, 1849
Lincoln applied for a patent to help boats through shallow waters. The patent was granted on May 22.

February 1, 1850
Eddie Lincoln died.

December 21, 1850
William Wallace, the third Lincoln son was born.

April 4, 1853
Thomas Lincoln was born. He is best known as Tad.

April 27, 1853
The town of Lincoln, Illinois was named for him and he christened it with watermelon juice!

Spring 1856
The Lincoln Home was enlarged to two full stories.

December 1, 1856
Due to the absence of Judge David Davis, Lincoln presided over Sangamon County Circuit Court.

June 16, 1858
Lincoln accepted the nomination of the Republican party to run for U.S. Senate and gave his "House Divided" speech.

August 21, 1858
Running against Stephen Douglas for Senate seat, they held a series of debates in Freeport (August 27), Jonesboro (September 15), Charleston (Sept. 18). Galesburg (Oct. 7), Quincy (Oct.13) and Alton (October 15). Lincoln gave over 63 speeches during this campaign.

November 2, 1858
Lincoln won a majority of the popular votes, but Douglas was elected by vote in the legislature.

December 20, 1859
As interest rose in a Lincoln presidential candidacy, he sent his short autobiography to Jesse Fell.

February 27, 1860
Lincoln gave his famous Cooper Union address, which the New York Tribune printed in its entirety.

February 28, 1860
Lincoln began a 2 week speaking tour in New England. He stopped to visit his son Robert at Phillips Exeter Academy.

May 9-10, 1860
The Illinois Republican Convention supported Lincoln for President. Here he gained the nickname "The Rail Splitter."

May 18, 1860
With Lincoln back home in Springfield, he was nominated for President on the third ballot of the Republican Convention in Chicago.

October 19, 1860
Eleven-year-old Grace Bedell of Westfield, NY suggested that Lincoln grow a beard.

November 6, 1860
Lincoln became the first Republican to be elected President of the United States, defeating Stephen Douglas, John C. Breckinridge, and John Bell.

December 20, 1860
South Carolina seceded.

February 4, 1860
The Confederate States of America was formed and Jefferson Davis was inaugurated in Montgomery, Alabama, as President of the Provisional Confederate government. In February of 1862, he was inaugurated in Richmond, Virginia as President of the Permanent Confederate government.

February 11, 1861
Lincoln delivered his "Farewell Address" to the people of Springfield.

March 4, 1861
Lincoln was inaugurated the 16th President of the United States.

April 12-14, 1861
Fort Sumter was attacked by rebel forces and surrendered to the Confederates.

April 15, 1861
Lincoln called for 75,000 troops for three months.

July 21, 1861
In the evening, Lincoln learned that General Irvin McDowell's army had been defeated at Bull Run.

July 27, 1861
Lincoln placed General George B. McClellan in command of all troops in the vicinity of Washington.

November 1, 1861
Lincoln informed McClellan that he was to command the whole army.

February 6, and 16, 1862
Under General U.S. Grant, Union forces won at Fort Henry and Fort Donelson, on the Tennessee River.

February 20, 1862
Eleven-year-old Willie Lincoln died in the White House.

April 6-7, 1862
Union forces won at Pittsburgh Landing, Tennessee at the Battle of Shiloh, at great loss to both sides.

May 20, 1862
Lincoln approved the Homestead Act.

July 1, 1862
Lincoln called for 300,000 volunteers and approved the act providing a three per cent tax on incomes over $600.

July 2, 1862
Lincoln approved Morrill Land Grant College Act.

August 22, 1862
Lincoln wrote, "My paramount object in this struggle is to save the Union, and is not either to save or destroy slavery."

September 17, 1862
Gen. Robert E. Lee's invasion of the North is stopped by McClellan at the battle of Antietam or Sharpsburg, Maryland.

September 22, 1862
Lincoln read his preliminary Emancipation Proclamation to his cabinet.

November 5, 1862
Lincoln replaced McClellan with General Ambrose E. Burnside

December 12, 1862
Gen Burnside's Army of the Potomac is defeated at Fredericksburg, Virginia

December 31, 1862
Lincoln signed the bill allowing West Virginia to be a separate state in the Union.

January 1, 1863
Lincoln signed the Emancipation Proclamation declaring as free all slaves in the states in rebellion.

February 25, 1863
Lincoln approved act establishing national banks.

May 2-4, 1863
The army of the Potomac under General Joseph Hooker was defeated at Chancellorsville, Virginia.

June 27, 1863
General Hooker was relieved of command and replaced by General Meade.

July 1-3, 1863
The Confederate invasion of Pennsylvania under Lee was defeated by General Meade at Gettysburg.

July 4, 1863
General Grant's long siege of Vicksburg ended with Confederate surrender.

September 20, 1863
The Union army was defeated at Chickamauga Creek. Mary Lincoln's brother-in-law, General Benjamin Hardin Helm was killed at this battle.

November 19, 1863
Lincoln delivered the Gettysburg Address.

November 26, 1863
First Observance of Thanksgiving

March 10, 1864
Lincoln appointed General Grant commander-in-chief of all Union armies.

March 14, 1864
Lincoln ordered draft of 200,000 more men

June 28, 1864
Lincoln repealed Fugitive Slave Act.

July 18, 1864
Lincoln called for 500,000 volunteers

September 1, 1864
General Sherman occupied Atlanta, Georgia

November 8, 1864
Lincoln re-elected President.

December 19, 1864
Lincoln called for 300,000 more volunteers

December 22, 1864
Lincoln received the capture of Savannah, Georgia as a Christmas present from General Sherman.

March 3, 1865
Lincoln approved act establishing the Freedman's Bureau for care of ex-slaves.

March 4, 1865
Lincoln delivered his Second Inaugural Address, "with malice toward none; with charity for all."

April 4-5, 1865
Lincoln visited the evacuated city of Richmond, Virginia

April 9, 1865
General Lee surrendered to General Grant at Appomattox Court House.

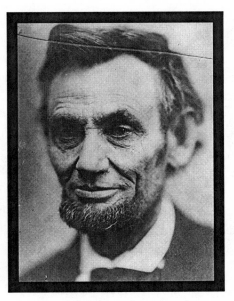

Lincoln's last photograph

April 11, 1865
Lincoln gave his last speech from window of White House in which he planned to restore the Union.

April 14, 1865
Lincoln was shot by John Wilkes Booth at Ford's Theatre.

April 15, 1865
Abraham Lincoln died at 7:22 AM .

April 19, 1865
Funeral services were held for the President in the White House.

April 21-May 3, 1865
Funeral train, carrying the bodies of President Lincoln and his son, William, returned to Springfield, Illinois.

May 4, 1865
Lincoln was interred in Oak Ridge Cemetery, Springfield, Illinois. Willie was interred with his father.

July 15, 1871
Tad Lincoln died and was buried with his father.

October 15, 1874
Dedication of partially completed Lincoln Tomb.

November 7, 1876
Three men attempted to steal Lincoln's body, thinking they would get rich on a large ransom.

July 16, 1882
Mary Lincoln died in the home of her sister Elizabeth Todd Edwards in Springfield. Mary was buried with her husband and three sons.

June 16, 1887
Robert Todd Lincoln presented the Lincoln Home in Springfield to the state of Illinois.

June 17, 1931
The remodeled Lincoln Tomb was dedicated.

April 2005
Abraham Lincoln Presidential Museum dedicated in Springfield, Illinois.

Lincoln's First Inaugural Address
Closing paragraph

I am loath to close. We are not enemies, but friends. We must not be enemies. Though passion may have strained, it must not break our bonds of affection. The mystic chords of memory, stretching from every battle-field, and patriot grave, to every living heart and hearthstone, all over this broad land, will yet swell the chorus of the Union, when again touched, as surely they will be, by the **better angels** of our nature.

Lincoln's Second Inaugural Address

At this second appearing to take the oath of the presidential office, there is less occasion for an extended address than there was at the first. Then a statement, somewhat in detail, of a course to be pursued, seemed fitting and proper. Now, at the expiration of four years, during which public declarations have been constantly called forth on every point and phase of the great contest which still absorbs the attention, and engrosses the energies of the nation, little that is new could be presented. The progress of our arms, upon which all else chiefly depends, is as well known to the public as to myself; and it is, I trust, reasonably satisfactory and encouraging to all. With high hope for the future, no prediction in regard to it is ventured.

On the occasion corresponding to this four years ago, all thoughts were anxiously directed to an impending civil war. All dreaded it--all sought to avert it. While the inaugural address was being delivered from this place, devoted altogether to saving the Union without war, insurgent agents were in the city seeking to destroy it without war--seeking to dissolve the Union, and divide effects, by negotiation. Both parties deprecated war; but one of them would make war rather than let the nation survive; and the other would accept war rather than let it perish. And the war came.

One eighth of the whole population were colored slaves, not distributed generally over the Union, but localized in the Southern part of it. These slaves constituted a peculiar and powerful interest. All knew that this interest was, somehow, the cause of the war. To strengthen, perpetuate, and extend this interest was the object for which the insurgents would rend the Union, even by war; while the government claimed no right to do more than to restrict the territorial enlargement of it. Neither party expected for the war, the magnitude, or the duration, which it has already attained. Neither anticipated that the cause of the conflict might cease with, or even before, the conflict itself should cease. Each looked for an easier triumph, and a result less fundamental and astounding. Both read the same Bible, and pray to the same God; and each invokes His aid against the other. It may seem strange that any men should dare to ask a just God's assistance in wringing their bread from the sweat of other men's faces; but let us judge not that we be not judged. The prayers of both could not be answered; that of neither has been answered fully.

The Almighty has his own purposes. "Woe unto the world because of offences! for it must needs be that offences come; but woe to that man by whom the offence cometh!" If we shall suppose that American Slavery is one of those offences which, in the providence of God, must needs come, but which, having continued through His appointed time, He now wills to remove, and that He gives to both North and South, this terrible war, as the woe due to those by whom the offence came, shall we discern therein any departure from those divine attributes which the believers in a Living God always ascribe to Him? Fondly do we hope--fervently do we pray--that this mighty scourge of war may speedily pass away. Yet, if God wills that it continue, until all the wealth piled by the bond-man's two hundred and fifty years of unrequited toil shall be sunk, and until every drop of blood drawn with the lash, shall be paid by another drawn with the sword, as was said three thousand years ago, so still it must be said "the judgments of the Lord, are true and righteous altogether"

With malice toward none; with charity for all; with firmness in the right, as God gives us to see the right, let us strive on to finish the work we are in; to bind up the nation's wounds; to care for him who shall have borne the battle, and for his widow, and his orphan- -to do all which may achieve and cherish a just and lasting peace, among ourselves, and with all nations.

"I felt sad and depressed at the downfall of a foe who had fought so long and valiantly, and had suffered so much for a cause, though that cause was, I believe, one of the worst for which a people ever fought."
General U.S. Grant – after Appomattox

"Abandon your animosities and make your sons Americans."
R. E. Lee, 1865

(Photo courtesy of Judith Duvall)

*A*fter 34 years of teaching, Betty Carlson Kay is enjoying her encore career, bringing history to life for children and adults. With ***The Civil War From A to Z,*** she offers viewpoints from each side of the conflict. Letters are explained first from the North's point of view, and then from the South's.

In honor of the 150th anniversary of the start of the Civil War in April 2011, Betty Kay will be visiting schools with a new one-woman presentation. This time, she will be three women whose lives were dramatically changed by the war, including Jennie Hodgers (AKA Albert Cashier), Mother Bickerdyke, and Julia Dent Grant. She is still available as Mrs. Mary Ann Rutledge, telling about Lincoln in New Salem, and as Mrs. Elizabeth Todd Edwards, above, telling the true story of her sister Mary Lincoln.

If your school is interested in a visit, contact Betty through her website at http://bckay.home.mchsi.com/

CPSIA information can be obtained
at www.ICGtesting.com
Printed in the USA
FFOW04n0343031017
40622FF